WHAT PEOPLE ARE SAYING

A practical guide to unlocking and repatterning one of the biggest mysteries of life — our mindset. Lynn has found a way to share her personal leadership journey with thoughtful and simple practices. The steps she lays out allows one to not only recognize how to navigate through difficult situations, but also how to prevent them through radical personal responsibility. Recognizing the role we play in the dynamics of our relationships in our professional and personal lives is one of the keys to unlocking our greatest potential. She offers us a gift by focusing on *your* growth and *your* awareness as well as the tools to be better leaders. This book is now one of the must-read workbooks that I use in my coaching and consulting practice with my executive clients.

— *Shushan Aleaqui, Executive Advisor and Leadership Coach*

There is elegance in the simplicity of assuming positive intent and Lynn's openness about her own journeys show leaders how to embrace that. *The Elegant Pivot* shows leaders that they don't need to be "sharks" to survive corporate politics; there is an easier approach to win and to bring everyone along with you.

— *Jason Cherry, Director, IS Technology Services*

Lynn Carnes has this way of sharing her experiences in anecdotes that are relatable, real, and hilarious. *The Elegant Pivot* is an invitation from Lynn to learn alongside her in moments of awkward high-stakes conversations, broken team dynamics, and so-absurd-they're-funny board room experiences. With *The Elegant Pivot*, Lynn has distilled how to bring our best selves forward, create richer, more authentic conversations, and build teams on a firm foundation of trust because we assume the positive intent in ourselves and in others. I highly recommend this book and all of Lynn's work.

— *Michele Stowe, Founder of SkyRocket Coaching LLC*

The Elegant Pivot sounds like an optional move, but don't be fooled. The practices in this enlightening book are mission-critical for any leader who wishes to create positive change and sustained followership. This book should be required reading for any leader who wishes to lead inclusively. We don't get far with others without assuming positive intent. The work begins with us. The practical wisdom of *The Elegant Pivot* is necessary for anyone wishing to lead in today's complex and dimensionally diverse world of work.

— *Susan MacKenty Brady, CEO, Simmons University Institute for Inclusive Leadership, Deloitte Ellen Gabriel Chair for Women and Leadership, Author,* **Mastering Your Inner Critic**

Loved this read. I spent time with Lynn during some of the times she references and I can honestly say the skill of assuming positive intent has and continues to frame how I respond to what I experience in the world. As a Black man, I use assume positive intent to deal with my possible emotional responses to inequities that I experience. What Lynn's book taught me was that in addition to using this tool, I need to re-engage by asking a question to create a learning moment for both parties. Thanks for the lesson, Lynn.

— Vernon Roberts, Founder and Principle of
Evoke Virtual

Read this book — it is a gem. *The Elegant Pivot* is a practical, straightforward guide with loads of wisdom distilled from years of hard-earned experience. For those of you who have found value in other works in the field of personal leadership development, you will see themes like "growth mindset," "emotional intelligence," and "daring greatly." And if this is the first book you've picked up on the topic, you should keep reading. *The Elegant Pivot* builds on and integrates these and many other ideas in a wonderfully accessible way. It carries you forward and when you finish reading it, you will have expanded your perspective and capacity as a professional and as a leader. It will also help you find the joy in your work.

— Katy Strei, EVP and Chief Human Resource
Officer at Emergent BioSolutions

I have known Lynn for over twenty years as both a professional colleague and a trusted friend. I can bear witness through direct observation and shared stories to many of the experiences and anecdotes she shares as she demonstrates "positive intent assumed." Her simple, yet remarkably powerful heuristic approach to transforming unproductive habits into positive methods leads to extraordinary results, in contexts ranging from corporate leadership to personal relationships. Lynn's approach pivots a common negative notion about making assumptions by starting with a focus on positive outcomes."

—*Steve Snyder, CAPT, US Navy (ret), Adjunct Professor, Regent University*

Lynn gives valuable interesting perspectives on how to communicate and interact with others. This helps to organize thoughts and behavior when dealing with others.

—*Hank Steinberg President, Steinberg & Associates, Inc.*

Lynn Carnes does not disappoint. She captured my attention in the very first sentence of this book. She has coached me in the art of assuming positive intent. It has changed my life. If you read this book it will change yours.

—*Carolyn Swinton, Chief Nursing Officer, Prisma Health*

The "Assume Positive Intent" strategy is one of the most powerful tools I have ever learned. It enables you to own your power in *any* situation. While you may not be able to control what happens in life or with other people, this tools allows you to transform any situation so that it works *for you*. I believe it to be a human superpower, that when invoked, unlocks an array of other powerful tools that ultimately lead to the result you choose. It also affords others a charitable assumption that I hope they will afford me.

— Jenny Isgett, Esq.

Lynn is a born learner — and teacher. In the style of Molly Ivins, she takes us to the board room, the alpine slopes, and the ski boat to regale us with humorous and relatable stories of human foible. When tensions are rising and we assign motive to others without first validating it, we're often off base. Lynn shares her discovery about a better way to leverage those tensions, with often surprising results.

— Kira Higgs Principle, Straight Talk Strategy

This is the book I wished I had when in corporate America. *The Elegant Pivot* tells so many familiar stories and provides clear guidance for how to have difficult conversations. As Lynn notes in the book, we all need superpowers, and assuming positive intent can be a superpower.

— David Morales, Founder and CEO of
Neoclassical Builders, LLC

I've had the pleasure of calling Lynn both my friend and mentor for many years. The wisdom she shares in this book, I have learned from her first-hand and it has made a positive difference in my professional and personal life. Everyone in any facet of life would greatly benefit from reading this book.

— *Michelle Yelton, Director of Marketing &*
Communications, Tryon International Equestrian
Center & Resort

The Elegant Pivot is undeniably relatable. Carnes' words and stories illustrate the complexities of human nature and the human mind. Her ability to guide readers through introspection and practices of assuming positive intent will leave them feeling empowered and humbled in their work and in their personal lives.

Chelsea Mills, Mindset Coach

"Practicing the turn," as Lynn so eloquently states as the "elegant pivot," has been crucial in my success at assuming positive intent and thereby changing the relational story. Having had a tough start in life, I grew up defending myself so as to prevent further pain. I learned the hard way as an adult that always defending no longer served me well; rather it more often than not created much heartache and relational brokenness in the long-run. Working with Lynn in corporate America and as a private coach, I learned much from her regarding this strategy and have spent years practicing it with positive outcomes. *The Elegant*

Pivot brings to life how critical this strategy is in day-to-day living. Using her years of experience along with wonderful anecdotes describing practical application, she guides the reader on an engaging journey of how this concept of assuming positive intent can be the elegant pivot in any situation to create a new story. Not only will this resource be useful in the business arena, but I will utilize her work in my counseling ministry as a way to help individuals and families see a new way of relating which is productive rather than destructive.

—*Elizabeth Brooke, M.Div. Formation Director,*
Church of the Redeemer

The Elegant Pivot demonstrates what an excellent coach Lynn truly is: she provides information about workplace conundrums with solutions that are compassionate and actionable. In this age of the pandemic, while working remotely, it is more important than ever for corporate executives to learn to navigate workplace relationships successfully. Without face-to-face interactions with co-workers and teams, it is easy to fall into a trap of assuming negative intent. Lynn's laser focus on ways to find positive intent will forever change your business mindset and put you on an affirmative career path.

Julie Gould, Former President, Mercy
Community Capital

I had the good fortune to be coached by Lynn Carnes many years ago. When she introduced me to the idea of "assuming positive intent," it seemed like madness to someone whose decisions were always made from a place of self-preservation. Lynn helped me see that by making myself the victim of those whom I assumed were out to get me, I was avoiding taking responsibility for my own choices. This was life-changing.

— *Carl Baldwin, Conflict Resolution Specialist and Coach*

A perfect follow up to her first book *The Delicate Art: Learn to Say No and Unleash Your Performance*, Lynn gives us all a great strategy to manage our ever-changing environments. "The Elegant Pivot" reminds us all that the power of choice and the ability to adjust is the key to happiness and success in both our personal and professional worlds. A great read!

— *Tammy Tappan, Artist*

THE ELEGANT PIVOT

An Inspired Move for
Navigating Corporate Politics

LYNN CARNES

Carnes & Associates, Inc./Publishing Division
PO Box 127
Lake Lure, NC 28746

Paperback ISBN 978-1-7332171-2-5

Kindle ISBN 978-1-7332171-3-2

First Edition

Printed in the United States of America

CONTENTS

PREFACE

Many years passed before I learned the difference between operating from external strength forged from angry armor and internal strength fueled by something more curious and courageous.

In the late '90s, the armor I had created became the hologram of a corporate warrior, ever on the hunt for danger and ready to fight when the stakes were high. This hologram was like my second personality — one I lovingly referred to as Betty the Bitch. She conveniently handled the messy business of corporate life while letting the kinder parts of my personality completely off the hook. At least that's what I told myself. This alternate personality was uncovered after doing an exercise in *The Artist's Way*, by Julia Cameron. Of course, in my mind, I was more like Wonder Woman, fighting off the bad guys with my bullet-deflecting bracelets and roping people into doing things my way.

Approaching life armed for battle fueled my faux strength in the corporate world. It provided a shield for my soft and squishy inner world. Betty the Bitch was a handy, adult disguise for the scared little girl playing in the big leagues. Working in a large bank, I needed power and playing hardball seemed like the best way to get it.

As I climbed the ladder to "success," every promotion led to more responsibility, which led to more status, more money, and more time in the spotlight. Ever notice how light has a way of catching shadows? I didn't want to see them, even though they were chasing me around every corner. Ironically, I could see the shadow of everyone else.

It took a lot of breakdowns before I finally owned up to the reality of Betty's impact. My dark view of the world not only colored my reality, it became my reality.

I did not like living this way, but I could see no other way to live.

The corporate world truly is dangerous. Corporate politics can be played clean and it can be played dirty. Clichés have a way of capturing truth — and it was a dog-eat-dog world.

This book tells the story of another way to operate in the corporate arena — one that seemed incredibly preposterous to me at the time. Rather than attack and defend, the new move was a pivot, where I would give and take, fueled by seeing the world in a whole new way. The beauty of this move was that it worked in all circumstances.

There was just one catch. The move required me to drop my false armor so that I could tap into real, authentic strength. What the other players in my dog-eat-dog world were thinking or doing did not determine the outcome. With this simple pivot, *I* could influence the outcome. Even when every bone in my body was screaming to attack or defend, there was another choice that gave everyone a chance to be their best.

All I had to do was to "assume positive intent." It was an elegant move in the face of apparent danger. Simple. Graceful. Ingenious. Uplifting. There was just one problem — me.

My first, second, and third responses to this idea was to be expected, given the world as I knew it. No, NO, NOOOO! No way in hell was I dropping my armor. It seemed to be my only protection. Yet with some experience and experiments, I realized I was wrong.

What I thought would take away my power in a world of darkness turned out to be the most powerful tool I would ever have. Assuming positive intent turned out to be the go-to strategy when tempted to be judgmental, take something personally, or otherwise get self-protective or defensive.

When I first learned to assume positive intent, it was the situations that presented true harm that most concerned — *and confused* — me. Why would I make myself even more vulnerable than I already was? Why would I assume positive intent in cases where there was unequivocally NO positive intent whatsoever?

With lots of practice and more than a few missteps, it became evident to me that assuming positive intent kept me on the high road. It provided me with a full repertoire of possible strategies to apply. It kept me from being an unwitting player in the other person's game.

More times than I can count, I focused on the anger or self-interest or untrustworthiness of another person. This approach almost always ended up causing me more harm than the other person. No matter how justified it seemed to call them out for their egregious behavior, somehow, I was the one who got burned.

The elegant pivot allows us to "catch ourselves and respond" in a way that informs our actions and allows us to discern "the signal," focus on what we want, take nothing personally, and pen better stories.

The sequence for me goes something like this:

Pause - Assume Positive Intent - Get Curious - Ask a Question

The first three steps are internal. They are the "catch" that gets me ready for the pivot. Once I've gone through those steps, it's time to "respond." Start with a question or two. Rather than leaping to a conclusion, take a step back and gather more data.

In almost every story where assuming positive intent made the difference, the pivot happened around a question—just a simple question.

The sequence above appears so simple. Until, that is, we try to put it into action.

We humans are complex beings. If a simple question can turn everything around, then why is it so damn hard to summon the right question at the right moment? Why must I be curious when it's obvious what's going on? Why would I assume positive intent with someone who clearly has negative intentions? And why the hell would I pause when every cell in my body is demanding action and screaming danger? Why indeed.

Like a figure skater elegantly gliding across the ice, what appears so effortless on the surface was earned through many falls and failures. Oliver Wendell Holmes once said, "For the simplicity on this side of complexity, I wouldn't give you a fig. But for the simplicity on the other side of complexity, for that I would give you anything I have."

It comes down to a matter of trust. Do I trust myself to rise to the problem or do I depend on everyone else not to be the problem? Counting on the world to never inconvenience or offend me is a fool's gambit. Problems are going to happen. Anytime it feels like someone has done me wrong, it is natural for survival mode to kick in. The defenses have to come up. They just don't have to STAY up.

Assuming positive intent gives me access to my own problem-solving skills. It also gives me access to my hidden, often faulty assumptions, providing me with the opportunity to learn something about myself.

Some lessons are best learned the hard way. Learning to trust myself to operate from my internal strength and resources has come through a series of experiments, missteps, embarrassments, and downright failures.

This book is an invitation for you to join me in all the fun.

Before you decide that assuming positive intent is preposterous at worst or only for certain situations at best, consider this: No matter what just happened, the next line in the story has yet to be written. The very moment you most want to react from your own armor, crafted from your old habits, is actually the moment that allows for a turning point in the story.

By assuming positive intent, you see the bigger picture. I've been teaching this strategy to my coaching clients for more than 20 years, even as I was learning them myself. The question I hear most often starts with, "But what about...?" as the client describes a situation where someone is playing politics, acting selfishly, or is clearly out to get them. It's at these moments where we learn together just how many possible moves they really have. These new options are only revealed after they untangle their own assumptions.

On the surface, those three words, "assume positive intent," look like one thing—simple. Put in practice, however, it can be quite complex. Much more is going on than meets the eye. Through my many falls and failures, I've come to realize that assuming positive intent truly does give me the opportunity to write the next line in the story.

With practice, assuming positive intent becomes the "elegant pivot" that avoids broken relationships, navigates conflict, and turns the outcome in a new direction. It's easier said than done.

SECTION I

INTENTION HAS A CHARGE

Intention is a mysterious thing. It's this invisible force that has the power to make great things happen. Intention can also be extremely harmful.

Like electricity, it all depends on how you harness the force.

Electricity is one of my favorite forces of the modern world. Recently I passed a crew of technicians replacing power poles without shutting off the electricity. These technicians were using big orange insulators designed to keep the electric current from killing them. Because they understand its principles and have dozens of safety practices, and rules, and they can effectively utilize methods for keeping the electricity running through the wires rather than through their bodies.

The energy of intention is like the unseen force of electricity, in that it can be harmful or even deadly unless properly harnessed. For the most part, we have learned how to tame electricity. It works beautifully for me as I am typing under lights in an air-conditioned building, listening to an app that plays birdsongs for me. However, if I were to stick a piece of metal in a nearby outlet, then I would definitely get shocked or worse.

Likewise, intention is a powerfully useful force in human

interactions once we learn the principles, safety practices, and rules that allow us to harness and direct that power in the proper way. With all this talk about intention, force, and mystery, you might think this is a book about visualizing and manifesting your destiny. It's not.

We all operate with intention. You have yours as does everyone else. When we assume that we know others' intentions as well as we do our own, it is like putting a metal fork in the electric outlet. Not knowing their intentions while believing we do is where all the trouble starts. The elegant pivot insulates us from making a situation worse and sets us up to create a better outcome.

Nowhere have I experienced more "trouble" than in my corporate career. From the first day I walked through the door of my new job, I realized that things were not always as they appeared.

Human dynamics had more to do with success and failure than the work itself. Corporate politics often seemed to matter more than the work we were doing. Fear walked those halls and yet the rules required that we pretend we were fearless.

We could speak up freely in meetings—as long as we agreed with the boss. We were expected to bring our best ideas to the table—as long as those ideas did not shake things up too much. Building trust was an absolute necessity and so was watching out for backstabbing.

What I did not know in those early years—what I wish I had

known—was that everything I thought I knew was deeply colored by my own experiences. Yes, people were playing politics, but I was also an unwitting participant. My self-awareness, on a scale of one to ten, was a minus one.

As a result, I made things worse for myself than they had to be. The unseen intentions of everyone around me seemed like dangerous territory and my reactions made them even more treacherous.

We all need ways of dealing with intention—our own and the assumed intention of others—that keep the "electricity" from running through our bodies and hurting us.

It is completely natural to attribute a motive to someone's behavior. It's virtually impossible to be accurate in that attribution. I'm going to say that again, because it's the critical belief behind being able to pivot. Just because you think you know someone's intention does NOT mean you are correct.

Since we have no way of knowing what informs another person's motives, it's easy to make wrong assumptions. We can then get burned because we touch the "live wire" instead of insulating ourselves by doing more discovery or allowing ourselves to be curious. Misunderstandings follow along with hurt feelings, anger, and breakdowns in relationships. It's safer to assume you don't know the motive. And here's perhaps the most important point: Even if you are correct beyond a shadow of a doubt concerning a negative motive, things will still work out better for you if you assume positive intent.

We are constantly encountering other people with motives and intentions that we cannot see. It happens at work, in the store, while we commute, and anywhere we encounter people.

Leaving the post office one day, I was involved in a somewhat strange incident. I was walking out with a pile of boxes in my arms. A local gentleman, whom I know more by sight than personally, was moving slowly, and he started to walk toward my car. My first thought upon seeing him was, "Wow, he has REALLY slowed down! I wonder if his health is failing." Then he started making motions—without any words. At this point, his actions were a mystery to me. It wasn't until later that I realized his hand movements were making the offer to help open my car door.

My confusion was fueled by two other factors. First, my husband was sitting in the front seat. Second, my Doberman was sitting at the window of the back seat. It is not a good idea for anyone to open that back door, as Xena will go full-on Doberman first, and ask questions later. (This includes family members!)

Since he was moving very slowly and I tend to move fast and he wasn't saying anything, I did not yield to his gestures at all. Suddenly, he said, "Well excuse me for trying to be helpful," and walked off in a huff. (And oh my, how his anger gave him speed!)

It was only a few seconds later that my conscious brain finally registered that he was offering to open the door of my car to help me with my packages.

I'm sure he picked up on my unspoken thoughts of *"Don't*

open that door! My dog will bite you!" and the other set of unspoken thoughts to my husband of "Hey, how about opening the door and taking these packages off my hands." But instead of understanding the mystery dog or otherwise reading my mind, it registered to him as a rude form of rejection. He attributed intention and motive to me that were completely off-base. I was just too slow to put all the pieces together until after he was inside the post office and I was already driving away.

He did not understand my intent—and he walked off in a huff. There was a time in my life when someone acting this way would have escalated into a shouting match. It was the kind of incident that would color the rest of my day. Hopefully this encounter did not ruin his. Thanks to the information I'm sharing in this book, it did not ruin my day, for lots of reasons:

- I did not attribute to him thoughts that I had no way of knowing.
- I chose not to take offense to a misunderstanding.
- I assumed positive intent.

Learning to assume positive intent has changed my life. It's almost a "superpower." In these times we are living in, we need superpowers. Just when we think we can slow down and take a breath, something new comes along. Change happens at a rate much faster than most of us can adapt. Just when we think we are in a groove; something throws us a curve ball. It rocks us back on our heels, making us feel off-balance. All the stuff coming at us activates our Survival Mode, where we go into Flight, Fight, or Freeze. These actions are designed to enhance our ability to stay alive in the face of danger. They are not designed to enhance relationships, solve complex problems, think creatively, or make effective decisions.

When we work with other people, it's a common habit for us to "put thoughts" in their heads. They take an action and we think we know why. At best, we have an informed guess. At worst, we are completely off-base.

The elegant pivot turns us from thinking we know everything to being interested in learning more. Assuming positive intent is the gateway to curiosity. Curiosity breaks that cycle and sets the conditions for us to find out the real story, instead of making up a reason someone is doing something. Assuming positive intent gives you a chance to bypass the danger of your own imagined stories and instead to listen to what is really happening.

Not only does this improve the quality of our relationships, it sets the conditions for more elegant solutions, true innovation, and decisions that stand the test of time. All of this becomes more accessible by assuming positive intent.

This is a book about the electric charge of everyone else's intention. It's a book about the tools that make it possible to navigate the intention of OTHERS by putting into practice the "safety standards," rules, and methods to keep your assumptions about other people's intentions from "electrocuting" you.

Along the way, you will also learn how your own intentions

impact how you see others. You will also understand that your intentions have multiple facets, some of which are not so friendly and thus may hide from view.

Assuming positive intent has been much more than a gateway to curiosity for me. I've been able to enhance my own self-awareness by using it as a pause button to buy me a moment to gather myself and bring forward my best response rather than my worst reaction.

Instead of operating as a victim to everyone else's agenda, or as the one who needs to control everything, assuming positive intent has allowed me the elegant pivot from being the victim of circumstances to become the co-writer of my life.

My intention for this book is to share stories of my experiences and experiments to spark your own thinking about the possibilities. You, too, are the co-writer of your life. When faced with a moment where the story could go in one direction or the other, you have the ability to pick up the pen and take the story in a different direction. Knowing how to use the elegant pivot to assume positive intent is your first move.

CHAPTER ONE

RESISTANCE IS FUTILE

The pressure and uncertainty that comes with change taught me how to assume positive intent. At the time, I was a leader in a large bank. We were doing a merger every year, although it seemed like a merger every week. While integrating the systems, teams, and cultures in the mergers, I was also developing a brand-new team. On top of that, I was still expected to do my regular day job, which had just been re-engineered, so no one had ever done this job before. I had a daughter in high school, a new husband, and we had just moved across the country into a "new" old house.

All this change was running me. I had no power over my own life.

I will tell you that I did not handle all the emotions and challenges well at all. My reaction was to get angry. Of course, in the corporate world, we called it "frustration." That's more socially acceptable. I was a leader in name only. I could not give or receive help. My classic response to anyone that needed help from me was to say some version of "Suck it up, buttercup." Through my overwhelmed eyes, I saw nothing but trouble. I was anything but helpful to my team, my daughter, my friends, or my family.

But here's the biggest problem I remember from that time in my life: I was so overwhelmed that I could not even see what was really happening. I was treading water with my nose barely above the waterline. The intense Survival Mode that marked every day was normal to me.

When anything went wrong, I thought I knew why. I made up all kinds of stories about why things were happening. The co-worker who disagreed in the meeting was out to get me. The boss who canceled the meeting either did not respect me or had decided to give my work to one of my peers. The employee who missed an important detail didn't care about his job. My daughter getting caught with cigarettes would make me look like a bad mother. Every grocery store clerk I encountered had a cold or flu and seemed to be determined to contaminate my food.

I was also quick to act on my "knowledge." I made it clear to anyone and everyone that they crossed me at their peril. "Now just a damn minute" came out of my mouth and then I would berate whoever had done whatever I thought it was they were doing to me. My daughter had to suffer through so many "just a damn minute" moments of pure embarrassment in the grocery store.

It never dawned on me that there might be a better way to handle — pretty much everything. I was simply following some invisible rulebook that told me what to do when things got tough.

I lived behind a huge wall of my own making designed to keep everything out—including more change and anything else I didn't want to face!

It was in this time frame that the tiniest seed of a different way was planted. I tell the story in my TEDx talk from 2015. I had taken my team offsite for both team-building and planning. The coaches working with our team were providing lots of guidance on navigating the multiple layers of complexity and the politics of the organizational culture. In other words, they were teaching us how to deal with a scary bunch of backstabbing people who seemed more interested in throwing obstacles our way instead of getting good work done. At least, that's how I saw it at the time.

It was in this meeting that they mentioned the principle of assuming positive intent. In my world at the time, my unconscious assumptions were that everyone's intentions were self-serving. My idea of leadership was based strictly on authority. There was no give and take, no listening, no assumption of anything positive. I wasn't even aware of the concept of assumptions.

I had spent a good part of my career building a series of defenses with which to operate in the corporate world. I took great pride in being the one of whom no one took advantage. They might as well have told me to open the doors to the fort and let the marauders inside to wreak havoc. It struck me as the most absurd, naive, juvenile, falsely positive, put-your-rose-colored glasses-on strategy that I had ever heard. Talk about giving your power away! In my mind, no grown-up would ever think that assuming positive intent was a good idea.

Little did I know that doing so would be the MOST grownup thing to do.

The team and the consultants spent a lot of time in discussion over this topic. I pushed back and argued that assuming positive intent was just a lie. We owed it to ourselves and everyone else to see things as they were and to operate based on the truth.

The consultants gave us a mini teaching session on what it meant to assume positive intent. Whatever they said that day was lost to the steam coming out of my ears. I had hired these clowns and they were teaching my team to destroy me and setting me up for failure. I was doing anything but assuming positive intent.

Notwithstanding my very vocal resistance to the idea, the team decided it would not only be a good principle to practice for managing through the chaos of change — it would be a good team value. Against my wishes, we left the meeting that day with a new set of stated team values and a commitment to call each other out when we didn't assume positive intent.

The woman who was overwhelmed and living behind a self-protective wall of her own making was thrown a lifeline — if only I would take it!

I had my first chance — it was really a test — on the way home from that meeting. Thanks to bad weather, my flight home from that meeting got diverted to an unfamiliar city, where I would have to spend the night in a hotel near the airport. As a veteran traveler, I knew the cab driver would be unhappy to get such a short fare. But I was too tired to wait for the hotel bus, so with a twinge of guilt, I hopped into the first taxi in line.

The cab ride for the airport hotel seemed way too long and soon I was conjuring up the story that he was extending the miles to pad his fare. I was steaming by the time we pulled into the hotel. Now it was time to pay the fare.

Should I call him out for cheating me?

Should I just be quiet and pay him his fare and a tip?

Should I just pay him only his fare and say nothing?

It never occurred to me to just ask why it took so long. With the lesson of assuming positive intent still ringing in my head, internally, I said "Fine" and handed him his full fare and tip without saying anything. In the back of my mind, I wondered if I had just been cheated. Secretly, I wanted to prove to my team and those coaches that they were wrong.

The next morning, I planned to take the bus back to the airport for my flight. As I looked out my hotel room window, the airport filled my view . My fear of being cheated flared up and I was pretty sure that assuming positive intent had just burned me. I was so mad! *Never again*, I said to myself. Those coaches and my team are "full of it." I will NEVER assume positive intent again. (Mind you, this was all overspending $10 on a cab fare — but I will save my cheap mindset for another story.)

Then I got in the hotel shuttle bus for the longest short ride to the airport of my life. While the hotel was near the airport, the route to enter the airport was on the other side — it was a good 15 minutes from door to door. As the ride progressed, I started getting mad at the bus driver for taking so long. (Notice a theme here?) It took me a while, but I finally got it. This is how long it takes at this airport! No one was trying to screw me. By the end of the ride, I was no longer angry; in fact, I was even relieved. Assuming positive intent in the first place would have saved me from getting angry and upset for no reason.

That simple incident planted a small seed that lay dormant for many years. For the longest time, I explained away the cab story as a lucky accident. Nothing in that experience gave me a way to handle difficult office politics, family dynamics, or big change.

However, my self-protective ways were not working either. I started reading between the lines that my team was losing respect for me. My marriage was on the rocks. My daughter was struggling deeply. Eventually I came to realize that something must change. Since it seemed the world out there would continue getting more complex and faster, it might be possible that I was the one who had to change. I really, *really* did not want to change. What I really wanted was for someone to give me an "A" or a gold star for gaining knowledge. I had read all the leadership books. I could espouse every theory. I "knew" a lot of stuff.

It changed nothing about how I approached the world. It

would take going much deeper for me to change. First, I had to admit that I might not know it all. I had to realize that my mind was making a lot of leaps that were not necessarily accurate. My fears were driving almost every action. Fortunately, another coach came along who started encouraging me to look deeper. She showed me that just because I had a habit of doing things one way did not mean I had to keep doing it that way forever. There was just one catch. I would have to look at myself, and how I made sense of the world. Damn. Looking at my beliefs, assumptions, and my own intentions scared the hell out of me.

CHAPTER TWO

A BETTER HABIT

Always looking for negative intentions in others is a habit—not unlike smoking, nail biting, or eating candy. These old habits were developed for good reasons. People are complex. We have more than one intention at any given time. The investment advisor wants to help you make more money and he wants to make more trades that boost his income. The co-worker wants to do her best work and she is feeling insecure and wants to get more credit than you do. The person on your team who seems so obstinate is really trying, but afraid he'll never be good enough. Your boss really wants you to do well and he's also concerned that you might not be paying attention to all the necessary factors.

For me, looking for negative intentions was a self-protective, "I'm going to get you before you get me" kind of habit. What I did not realize was that focusing on the negative only made things worse.

The best way to change a habit is not to stop it, but to do something differently. That's where having a go-to strategy helps. Assuming positive intent is the go-to strategy when tempted to be judgmental, take something personally, or otherwise get self-protective or defensive.

Our brains are designed to look for danger. It's a part of our hard-wired Survival Mode. When we are faced with the complex mix of the intentions people show us and the intentions they don't, our automatic habit is to assume the worst. It feels so much safer.

Once we get a whiff of what we interpret as negative intentions, it becomes difficult, if not impossible, to see anything else. Our brains tell us we must deal with the danger in front of us, and so we instinctively proceed from a defensive posture.

Instead of protecting us, looking for danger actually creates more danger.

In the electricity analogy, it's as if we all have multiple "wires" of intention. Some of the wires represent positive intentions. Others are more negative or self-serving intentions. Touching the positive wires is safer, leads to being curious, allows us room to listen, and gives us a more complete picture of what is really happening. Touching the negative wires can often send the electric current right back into us.

We would be foolhardy to ignore the fact that people have multiple intentions. Assuming positive intent doesn't mean we are blind to the humanness of others, or unaware of genuinely negative intentions.

We would also be foolhardy to believe we know everything that is happening and why. It's human nature to jump to conclusions. It takes work and discipline to dig deeper and fully understand the situation. Almost always, even when we do fully understand the situation, assuming positive intent is still the best move, for reasons that will become clear as we unpack it.

Early in my exploration, I came across "The Ladder of Inference," which is a way of understanding why it so difficult to challenge our own assumptions. Peter Senge's book *The Fifth Discipline Fieldbook* describes it this way: "We live in a world of self-generating beliefs which remain largely untested. We adopt those beliefs because they are based on conclusions, which are inferred from what we observe, plus our past experience."

In other words, there is much more happening than the sequence that we see: "I get data." "I take action." Many steps occur between those two; however, they are typically happening outside of our awareness. The Ladder of Inference shows us the "rungs on the ladder" we take between information and action.

From the moment we get our first piece of data, we are already missing something. Our human perception simply cannot take in everything. So, before we have even made a conscious choice, our mind has selected a subset of the data on which to focus. Thanks to our filters, the only things you will notice are the things that you have consciously or subconsciously decided matter the most.

The first time I heard the idea of filters, the person describing it called it the "yellow Volkswagen syndrome." When was the last time you saw a yellow Volkswagen? At the time, I could honestly say never. So, he challenged me to be able to say the same thing within a week. "You watch. You might see one on the way home tonight." Frankly, I thought he was full of it. How could I have missed something so obvious?

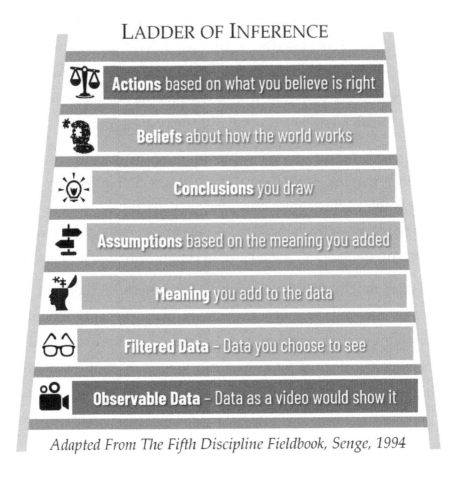

LADDER OF INFERENCE

Actions based on what you believe is right

Beliefs about how the world works

Conclusions you draw

Assumptions based on the meaning you added

Meaning you add to the data

Filtered Data – Data you choose to see

Observable Data – Data as a video would show it

Adapted From The Fifth Discipline Fieldbook, Senge, 1994

Clearly, I was filtering myself from my own ignorance about filters. Sure enough, I saw a yellow Volkswagen on my way home from work. Then I saw another and another. Suddenly, yellow Volkswagens were everywhere. They had been there all along; now that my filter was primed to see them, I couldn't miss them. It's been a gift that has lasted for a very long time. I've been seeing yellow Volkswagens ever since.

We can assume that for every open "filter" we have, there are many more that are closed. The best we can do as mere mortals is to take in a subset of all the possible information available to us. Knowing that we must be missing something opens the door to the awareness of the rest of the steps on the Ladder. It also opens the door to curiosity.

The next rung on the Ladder is where we add some form of *Meaning*. It is very difficult to see data and not ascribe some meaning to it. It's essential to our survival, and we are hard-wired to tune into threat first.

Example: Someone looks at their watch. Does it mean that they are late? That they are bored? That it vibrated to remind them of something? Unless we are aware and disciplined, we will automatically choose the possibility that points to the highest threat.

Even with awareness and the intent to catch ourselves first, the potential meanings for such a glance are numerous. The meaning we assign to it comes from our experience. Somewhere, somehow, we assigned meaning to the glance at the watch. That meaning comes from our personal history, our culture, and the values we were taught.

BOB'S STORY

I end the meeting and excuse myself before getting to the point

Bob can't be trusted to hear me out

Bob thinks I'm wasting his time

Bob wishes he hadn't taken the meeting

Bob is feeling impatient

Bob glances at his watch

Bob and I have an important meeting. I wasn't sure he would meet because he's said he had no time before. We're in a conference room next to a busy hall, with a loud conversation next door. Bob's wife is expecting and has an important doctor's appointment. Bob started to speak, then stopped and glanced at his watch. I'm getting to the most important points and the words are hard to find. Bob has an iWatch. And there are many, many other details...

The watch example is relatively neutral. However, what happens when the meaning we assign has bigger consequences? One day, I was sitting in a meeting with coaching client Cody. His boss, Guy, had hired me to be his coach, and knew we were meeting in one of the conference rooms.

When I take on a coaching client, one of the commitments I ask of the client and the manager hiring me is to treat coaching time as sacred. It's also quite common for me to hold that space

24

as a higher priority than my clients until we have a few opportunities for it to be tested. It was about to be tested.

About one third of the way into our meeting, Guy tapped on the door and interrupted us. Hmmm. That action indicates this might be a big deal. It was not long after the 911 terror attacks, so interruptions like this elicited more fear and apprehension than usual. Nonetheless, my assumption was that Guy would only interrupt us for something very important, something that superseded both our agreement and the inherent importance of coaching.

Instead, it was a simple moment that turned into a lifetime of learning for Cody—and for me. Guy gave an assignment to Cody, and Cody said okay. The assignment appeared to be a simple task easily done later from my vantage point. So when Guy left the meeting, I prepared to resume . I certainly did not expect Cody to leave and lose his coaching time. Cody thought otherwise.

Before I could say anything, Cody looked at me and said "While he didn't say it, Guy expects me to stop what I'm doing and get that done for him. Should take me about 15 minutes and I'll be back."

As he got up to leave the room, I said "Before you make that assumption, can we check it out?" Cody's face fell and I sensed he was reluctant. Just this little pause started the clock ticking on the assignment. With my question, he had a choice between two priorities: Follow the lead of his coach or his boss. What would it be?

I asked Cody if he were willing to "go live" in his coaching and test his *Assumption* about the timing of Guy's request. As I listened to the earlier exchange, it struck me that Cody had listened and agreed to the request without asking about timing. Since Guy's office was just down the hall, I suggested that instead of going back to his desk and quickly getting the request done, he find Guy and ask him for clarification on *when* he wanted the task done. Cody agreed, and I waited alone in the conference room.

Very quickly Cody returned. It turned out that Guy did not need the task done so quickly; in fact, it could wait for up to a week!

We spent the rest of his coaching time debriefing the lessons from this experience. Cody jumped from "boss interrupted a meeting" to "immediate action" because in his mind the *Meaning* of such an interruption was directly linked to his **Meaning of authority**. In general, Cody did what the boss asked, no questions asked. It was something he had learned from his task-master father. After Cody entered the workforce, he treated his bosses the same as he did his dad.

The next rung on the Ladder of Inference is the *Assumption* we make based on our personal Meaning. In this case, Cody assumed that the boss's request took priority.

Very quickly, we move from the rung of *Assumption* to the rung of our *Conclusion*. It's virtually instantaneous. Cody concluded that his best move at that moment was to take care of this request rather than continue our meeting.

This decision reinforced his *Belief* that the boss's request takes precedence over everything else. Short of having the good luck to have this interruption happen, he might never have questioned his reflexive *Actions* to managing the requests of this or future managers.

CODY'S STORY

Leaves an important meeting to do the task

Boss takes precedent over everything

Must do this now

Request is a priority

Boss has something super important

Everything happening inside / outside of meeting

Cody sees his boss, feels urgency

At every stage on the Ladder of Inference we are adding something to the data. Going through the Ladder of Inference in Cody's story looked like the preceding graphic (bottom to top).

It's human nature to jump to *Conclusions*. It's a habit shared by almost everyone, and it's so normal that we don't even see it as a habit. Most of our steps from *Data* to *Action* are happening in the blink of an eye, and it's an internal process. All but the top and bottom rungs on the Ladder are what happens internally within us.

The brain likes certainty much more than uncertainty. That's why we move through the steps of the Ladder of Inference at light speed. The sooner we can resolve the tension the better.

With lots of repetition, we can train ourselves to slow down and develop a new habit. Even when we start to focus on training for a new habit, our Survival Mode kicks in to do the "Let's keep you safe" thing. It takes focus, discipline, and attention to retrain our ingrained reactions.

Assuming positive intent gives us permission to pause, allowing our attention to catch up with our reactions. It shifts us away from an agitated state to a "fascinated state." It also buys us time to help the other person do the same. That's right. The other person in the story has a Ladder of Inference as well. In Cody's story, his boss was climbing up his own Ladder of Inference and so was I. We are all doing it all the time. It's a common, human habit that very often keeps us from seeing our choices. We tend to think our interpretation of what is happening is JUST THE WAY THINGS ARE.

Notice that the Ladder of Inference that we follow is mostly informed by our past. **When we jump to Conclusions, we rarely**

realize that we have really jumped into our past. Suddenly, we are not solving the problem that is in front of us; we are focusing on out-of-date knowledge that we most likely acquired as children. Our selective focus ends up creating a new problem by missing the subtle cues of the present moment.

Contrary to my early belief, it turned out not to be a falsely positive thing at all. Assuming positive intent now sparks my curiosity, which keeps my attention on solving the problem rather than needing to be self-protective or trying to look good. When I'm curious, I have a much better chance of staying in the moment and discovering what is really happening in front of me. **Curiosity is a mental tool that allows me to break the trance of my past and opens me to seeing the complexities and truth of the present situation.**

Assuming positive intent also challenges me to pay attention to my own weaknesses and vulnerabilities. When I can't assume positive intent, (and there are still many, many times where I find it difficult or impossible) I can trace it to something I am still working on within myself. It has become a priceless mirror for self-awareness.

At the simplest level, assuming positive intent allows me to respond rather than react. Being on the defensive just creates more need to be defensive.

At a deeper level, when I only see the negative, I can be sure something important in myself that I don't want to face has taken control of my actions. This kind of insight has given me a window into better understanding and healing old hurts and correcting biases.

Regardless of my level of personal growth, some situations are easier to handle than others.

Context matters. The following chapters provide practical illustrations for assuming positive intent in different contexts. There are different levels of engagement that we have with people. These chapters cover four basic situations where you might find assuming positive intent a useful way to deal with the situation. And just for fun, I'm giving the people in these situations some descriptive names.

The Uninvolved: Just Minding Their Own Business. Let's call him "Blameless Bobby". He is just going through his day, doing his thing, having no intention to bother you one way or the other.

The Innocent: They Really Didn't Mean Anything by It. "Accidental Annie" might say or do something, completely unaware that she is pushing your buttons or getting your goat.

The Provocative: They Might Have a Point. "Provocative Peter" intentionally challenges you. Whether he is an "attacker" remains to be seen. How you respond likely determines which path he follows.

The Attacker: They Really Do Mean You Harm. "Fighting Francis" may be the most challenging of all. She is definitely out to get you and she will do anything to get her way, while making things go poorly for you.

These situations get increasingly difficult to navigate. Your actions can take a Blameless Bobby to a Fighting Francis in a split second. Anyone who has encountered road rage can relate. If you go through life spoiling for a fight, I promise you this: you will get plenty of fights! I know this because I did it.

You can certainly justify NOT assuming positive intent, especially when encountering a Provocative Peter or a Fighting Francis. There are going to be people in your life who are not operating with positive intent. Yet ironically, the best strategy in most cases is to still assume positive intent. Sound crazy? That's what I thought too.

THE UNINVOLVED: JUST MINDING THEIR OWN BUSINESS

"Blameless Bobby"

The uninvolved people in our lives are those we encounter daily when we are out shopping, in traffic, walking down the hall at work, or traveling through the airport. The first assumption we can make with Blameless Bobby is that he did not get up in the morning having the intent to get in your way, be rude, or take advantage of you personally. You can safely assume the Blameless Bobbys of the world are going through their day just hoping to get through their daily challenges without too much trouble. The cab driver in my story above would fall into this category. When they do something annoying, if you assume positive intent and be kind, you can save yourself all kinds of counter-productive emotions and your day will likely be better.

In what could have been a minor and fleeting incident, I recall that I became acutely aware of this on a trip through the Denver airport back in the days when they had an "expert traveler" line. Being the business traveler that I was, and always in a hurry, I headed for the special Expert Traveler line expecting to find a similar group of businesspeople. What I found instead was a young mother and her small child in front of me. Immediately, I started having these nonsense thoughts in my head; *"What is she doing in this line? Does she not know that she is not an expert traveler? Did she not see the sign? Can we get someone over here to get her out of my way?"*

I was seconds away from creating a big old scene with the authorities when she did something that snapped me out of this nonsense. She put her child on the floor freeing her hands in order to manage her many bags. At first, I was shocked that a mother would be so careless as to put a child on the floor in such a place as the security line in the airport. Then it dawned on me that she was desperately trying to manage bags, a child, and the agitated woman behind her. Suddenly, I quit seeing an obstacle and instead saw a frantic mom just trying to get through the airport like everyone else. Something inside me shifted and I began to help her with her bags.

The new "story" tapped into my caring instead of my initial self-absorbed reaction. That shift in how I looked at the situation and reacted to it lasted through the remainder of the trip. I began seeing everyone in the airport as simply trying to get through the day in the best way they knew how. As a result, I was a kinder, gentler traveler, and the rest of the trip was much more pleasant.

The Blameless Bobbys of the world are everywhere — and they really are just trying to get through their day, just like we are. Assuming positive intent with the uninvolved people in our lives humanizes them and taps into our empathy. We can then see them as normal people doing the best they can, even when they seem to be making a mess of it. When you act on this story with caring and kindness, everyone's day is likely to go a little better.

Bottom line: We can safely assume that the uninvolved bystanders in our lives did not wake up planning to ruin our day.

CHAPTER FOUR

THE INNOCENT: THEY REALLY DIDN'T MEAN ANYTHING BY IT

"Accidental Annie"

The "innocent" people in our lives are those who say or do something that offends us or causes us to judge them harshly. Accidental Annies have no idea they did something to upset you. You might misread an expression on their face. Or the email you think they didn't respond to is sitting in your spam folder. You learn later that it was actually a family crisis, not rudeness, that accounts for the unanswered text. There are many reasons we might get offended when in reality, the other person has absolutely intent to offend or any idea that they have.

So many cases of assuming negative intent start with an innocent player. For example, it's the norm when speaking in front of a group to assume the smiling person in the back of the room has positive intent. It gets a little more difficult when you can't read the expression on the boss's face, or you don't know someone well. In this case, it can be easy to assume something negative is happening behind that blank face. The same is true when speaking on the phone. It's easy to assume the worst when that uncomfortable silence comes after you have said something a bit provocative and suddenly the cell phone call drops.

When you perceive that someone or a certain situation is negative, it's incredibly useful to ask some probing questions before assuming the worst. Before concluding that someone is ignoring your email, pick up the phone and ask. Before taking something personally, ask yourself whether there might be another explanation. Before going down a retaliatory path for the lack of response to a text, make that phone call. Before assuming you know what someone is thinking by reading his or her face, just ask. Before getting angry over something someone said in all innocence, take a moment to assume positive intent.

My mind tends to make leaps that are totally off the mark when reading email. After sending a brand-new piece of work to a co-worker — without providing any context other than *"Can you take a look at this and let me know what you think? –* the first email back was a simple, *"Where is this going?"* That's it. My mind reflexively went to the worst place possible. My first thought was that she hated it and was hoping that no one had seen it yet. Then I thought *"Why doesn't she like it?"* and other such self-deprecating nonsense.

Before I let my stories run too wild, I called her and just asked, *"What's behind the question?"* The answer could not have been simpler. She merely wanted to know if this was going on the website or directly to clients. She loved it and just wanted to evaluate it in the context of its intended application. Boy was I glad that I hadn't acted on any of my stupid mind-trick stories!

An example of the importance of context happened when I was in a meeting with a coaching client, Jerry. He had received an email from his boss that simply said, *"Can you come see me this afternoon after 3:00?"* He was so upset by the email that he couldn't focus on our meeting with the rest of his team.

At the end of our meeting, he mentioned the email and his concerns. We went back to his office, where I asked him if I could read it. He turned the screen around and showed it to me, commenting that he could not believe the audacity of his boss.

After rereading all 9 words, I still didn't see what was so upsetting. Clearly, I was missing some context here. So, I asked him what he was concerned about. And he had lots of good reasons to be mad, all inferred from that one sentence.

He had chosen to assume that the simple words in the email were a sign that he had made a mistake. In the story he was telling me, the only reason the boss would ask him to come to the office was to read him the riot act about something he had done. However, if the boss just knew WHY he had done what he had done, the boss would not be mad.

"How sure are you that this is the situation to which your boss is referring?" I asked. "Well, what else could it be?" he retorted. Then I mentioned several other possibilities and he reluctantly acknowledged that yes, maybe, possibly it could be one of the other big projects he was working on.

I then asked him the most powerful question of all: *"What other possible stories would explain this email?"* After a couple of false starts, I witnessed a transformation that day. He kept talking and eventually came to realize that he needed a meeting with his elusive boss and that he had just received an invitation for the very thing he needed. He changed his mind about how to plan for that meeting. We jointly crafted a way for him to position his topic, and I asked him to set aside the first situation unless the boss brought it up. He agreed. And you know what happened? To his relief and surprise, he got the result for which he was looking.

It's so tempting to tell ourselves stories that protect us, make us the victim, and make the other person the villain.

Based on our past experiences, we develop an "internal story" of our lives where we are the character, the narrator, and the writer all at once. We think we are looking at the facts. Indeed, the fact of the email was plain for all to see: *"Can you come see me this afternoon after 3:00?"* The first internal story Jerry told himself about the "plot" put him in a bad place. When he changed the story, he changed the outcome. The question *"What other possible stories would explain this email?"* gave him the space to check out the internal story.

Assuming positive intent FIRST gives you a moment to pause and check out your internal story before you act on it—and perhaps make a fool of yourself.

One of my favorite examples of this involved a team meeting

in which one of the members was introducing new software and tools in front of his team, including the boss. This was a very "visionary" recommendation, and he knew it was a risk to bring it up, especially since the current tools appeared to be working fine. As Carl described the tools and the resulting consequences of implementing this vision, he noticed his boss, Bob, with his head in his hands.

In this case, it was easy for Carl to assume the boss hated his idea, and that is exactly what he started thinking. While he was talking, he noticed these kinds of thoughts running through his mind: *"Bob hates this." "Bob is crazy if he doesn't agree with me." "Bob is so stupid – I should get another job." "This company never goes for daring ideas – I hate this place."* These thoughts happened in mere nanoseconds and did not really reflect how Carl felt about his company. After the internal chatter started, he noticed a defensive and then belligerent tone in his voice as he presented. Once he noticed, he had a choice. But would he pause and do something different or press on?

His first choice was to defend his idea. That path was by far the most tempting. After all, Carl was quite sure he was right and had the facts to defend his position. That path also risked picking a fight with Bob. His second choice was to back off and avoid the fight altogether. If he backed down now, the whole team would likely lose access to a better way of doing things. Importantly, there was a third choice and that's the one he decided to take.

He called for a break in the meeting. Carl took his boss aside and asked, "I've noticed some body language from you, and I don't know what it means. Could you tell me what you are thinking?" The answer from the boss shocked him. "I'm realizing that everything you are saying is the way we need to go. And that means I have to go sell it to my upper management, ask for more resources, and change the composition of our team. I'm just thinking through all the implications, which is making my head hurt!" Because Carl assumed positive intent and asked a question, the tone of the meeting stayed in problem-solving mode, and eventually, they did implement the new recommendation.

Had Carl acted on his initial assumption of the worst-case scenario, fueled by seeing his boss's head in his hands, it is highly likely the boss would have taken the easy route and stuck with the old plan.

Why is that? When we get defensive, it sets up a game of, "I'm right and you're wrong," and so creating two sides to the issue. In the above case, the boss was already on the side of the presenter. If the presenter had gotten defensive, chances are the boss would have become entrenched and taken the other side simply out of habit, regardless of the genuine value of the idea.

Remembering to assume positive intent interrupts the old pattern of thinking and gives us a chance to act on what's really happening, instead of operating from our fear-based thinking.

Here's another example from my personal life that I've never forgotten. When my daughter Jen was young, she asked me one day, "Mom, why are you mad?" I asked her what made her think I was mad. Her response, "You have on your mean face." Now I often felt angry and mean back in those days, but on this day, I was fine. Or so I thought.

I looked in the mirror and saw what she was talking about. Indeed, my face did look mean, with the eyebrows scrunched together. However, in that instance, I was just concentrating on something else. And I explained to her that was how I looked when I was thinking really hard.

Based on our history together, her assumption of anger on my part was fair. My daughter just assumed that her angry mother might be about to erupt. In this case, she asked. She is still asking to this day. She calls it "Mom Face." After watching myself on video, I've come to learn that I have a very expressive face. We have an agreement for her to ask me before assuming I'm mad. And I've promised myself to never play poker for high stakes.

Sometimes people just have a neutral or scowling face. (Some call this the resting bitch face—Google it. You will find some hysterical videos.)

If you assume the worst, you are likely to start behaving differently, and it's even possible to offend the other person. A quick way to assume positive intent is to think of the set of facts that would make the other person's behavior make sense. A gentle question about it can often keep you on a more positive path.

Bottom line: Ask questions before assuming you know how or what the other person is thinking or feeling.

THE PROVOCATIVE: THEY MIGHT HAVE A POINT

"Provocative Peter"

When we are living through and leading change, there is going to be disagreement and conflict. With so much uncertainty, we tend to want to move things into the "known bucket" as quickly as possible. Yet we need to be able to see all sides in order to get to the best answer for tough decisions. Provocative Peter gets louder than everyone else because he wants to make a point. You are having an honest disagreement about an idea. Possibly, he says something just to "get your goat" or assert power. He wants to get a rise out of you, or he is simply testing you. It's not that he is necessarily intending to cause you some sort of harm; he might just want to see what you will do.

Honest conflict around ideas and decisions falls into this category. Sometimes people have mixed emotions and feelings about a situation. In other words, the other person has BOTH positive and negative intent. I had a co-worker who knew that I hated to be late—and he frequently played on that fear by moving slowly or claiming I was late just to see what I would do.

He was definitely trying to get to me—and it was in that way close friends and buddies show love without being mushy.

We are complex beings, and we are often vacillating about how we feel about something, especially when the stakes are high. In most of these situations, it is fair to assume that the people around you are also experiencing a multitude of emotions and that they have conflicting points of view. This is especially true when leading change, making hard choices, and dealing with people. Whether you are working in a corporate setting with multiple change initiatives over a short period of time, or at home as the family tries to decide whether to move to take a new job, the Provocative Peters in our world seem to be everywhere, pushing and prodding us out of our comfort zones.

These are the circumstances where assuming positive intent can truly transform the situation and deepen relationships. If we are willing to see the many facets in play, and then touch those that bring out the best, we have increased our odds of staying on a productive path. Again, questions are a very useful tool to keep your mind from diving into the ditch.

In a moment of true illumination for me, I witnessed a co-worker completely transform a situation by assuming positive intent with a question. Our team had hired a consulting firm to do some design work and we were going to meet with the design team in their offices for the day. Being in a beautiful mountain location, both teams started the day with an early morning hike together. Our team decided to stop for breakfast on the way back to the office. The design team went back to get ready for the day.

The breakfast service was excruciatingly slow. However, our team leader Amy was unfazed and made the best of the situation by using the time for us work through some decisions and plan for some work. For us, the long breakfast turned out to be a big win. We were thrilled to have had the bonus meeting to make some decisions and get clarity on some work we were doing with one of our clients. That was until we got to the office.

As we got our coffee and started gathering in the meeting room, there was a definite chill in the air. Have you ever walked into a room where everyone suddenly got quiet and you could cut the tension with a knife? That's what we walked into. We initially assumed that the design team had been working through an issue and that our entry had interrupted an untimely fight among them. We were wrong.

The last person to come into the meeting room was Gary, the head of the design firm. We could all read the dark expression on his face. Personally, I wondered who was the object of his anger, still assuming that there had been a team conflict before we arrived. Little did we know that Provocative Peter was in the house.

As I sat there looking forward to getting started, Gary sat down and the mood in the room got even darker. He demanded an explanation. From us. About being late from breakfast.

Are you kidding me? This can't be happening! This situation had all the appearances of being a Fighting Francis. After giving an impassioned speech about how inconsiderate we were to waste his time like this, he started doing the regular check-in for the meeting, where we would go around the table and answer the question of the day.

Today's question was "Why do you think it was ok to be late?" Gary turned to his left and started the check in with one of my colleagues. Then he asked the next person at the table. And the next. Even though I was sitting far away, I held my breath.

It was clear that we were all going to get our chance to sit under his glare. Thanks to my position as one of the last to speak, I racked my brain for a good response. Clearly, Gary was out of line, but I could not think of a single response that didn't make things worse. I felt like asking Gary just who the heck he thought he was talking to, but that would have picked a fight. Several people contritely apologized like they were little children being scolded by daddy. That seemed to please Gary, but it also empowered his anger. Based on the deflated expressions on their faces, it also made grown people feel disempowered. Maybe that was Gary's intent? I wasn't sure.

When it was Amy's turn, she didn't blink, and she didn't wither under the stare. In a calm and respectful tone, she simply asked a question: "It seems like you are trying to make us feel bad for being late from breakfast. Could you tell me what you are trying to accomplish here?" Her even, neutral, curious way of speaking carried no judgment. It was like she was aware of the anger, but she chose to touch something else.

It was in this moment that we realized that Provocative Peter was not about to become Fighting Francis. Gary's reaction was like being snapped awake after sleepwalking. His expression and body language changed, and he immediately apologized and thanked her for her question. Everyone in the room felt the tension fall away and we all took a deep breath. Especially me, because I needed air, and now was off the hook!

We were quickly able to resume the meeting in a much more productive tone than where we had started.

I marveled at the turnaround that day and realized that I had just seen assuming positive intent in action. I was also aware that until we assumed positive intent, we did not know whether Gary was on our side or intending to derail us. Maybe assuming positive intent had some merit. I internally resolved to learn more about how to do it.

The key difference between Amy's response and the rest of us that day was taking Gary's comments personally. Amy didn't take the bait. The rest of us took it personally. We were either beating ourselves up for something that wasn't even wrong or judging Gary for being an ass or both.

Taking things personally can be like kryptonite to Superman. It makes us weak and open to attack. When we choose not to take things personally, we can focus on the next steps and what is really going on instead of trying to defend ourselves.

It can be very difficult to focus on the problem in front of us when we are feeling defensive. When the stakes are high, we tend to focus more on the consequences rather than taking it moment by moment. In one such case, my team and I were faced with unexpected pressure.

It was during a key project team meeting at the large bank where I worked at the time, and several of my team members (the ones who wanted to assume positive intent) were in the meeting. The opportunity was huge for us, as this was a high visibility project that could have made a positive difference to our clients at the bank and also would have been a game-changer for our own careers.

The executive sponsor had called the meeting to get an update. He had been extremely supportive until this fateful day. As we started presenting, he interrupted us several times with pointed questions. The expression on his face was grim. The questions seemed designed to trip us up. He was assuming anything but positive intent about what we were saying. Quickly, we concluded that he had done a complete turn around from everything he had previously supported. But why?

We felt like the rug had been pulled out from under us. As soon as we started getting the signals that he was no longer "on our side," we started selling, defending, and proving. We were no longer his colleagues; we were his subjects, hat in hand, asking him to grant us his favor again. He had all the power.

All of our selling and defending only made things worse. In that way that your future life can flash before your eyes, I had a picture of nothing but dark days ahead. We were digging ourselves into a deep hole. The project was about to be canceled! Then I would look bad, get fired, be homeless and starve to death on the streets. I often call this line of thinking "The Homeless Sequence."

I was picking an overpass to sleep under when, in a move of desperation, we called a break and huddled in a side room to regroup. We had NO consensus on how to move forward, and we were all somewhat afraid of what would happen if he actually did pull the plug on the project, or even worse—at least to our fragile egos—replaced us. Then someone said, *"What if we assume positive intent?"* My first reaction was the usual *"What a stupid idea."* While I didn't say those exact words out loud, everything in my tone, words, and body language communicated exactly that. Then someone asked, "What would explain his behavior that also fits the facts of the situation?"

We began answering that question and developed a different theory. When we actually looked at what he had said, everything came back to *"Why didn't I know about this?"* We had all told ourselves a story that explained that type of statement as "I don't like this." However, we asked ourselves this question: *"What if we interpret his question as meaning he would like to be more in the loop? How would we respond then?"*

This was hard to accept as a reasonable story, because he was a very senior executive and we were operating in a context where the folks at the top rarely rolled their sleeves up and got into the nitty gritty of a project. However, it was the best "assume positive intent" story we could make up and we had nothing else, so we went with it.

When we went back in the room, I said "Mark, our team just huddled to decide how to best address your concerns. We are getting the message that we have not kept you as informed as you would like. What would you like to see us doing more of to keep you in the loop?"

When I asked that question, he became animated and engaged and we realized in that instant that he was actually a bigger supporter than we had given him credit for. We simply needed to tell ourselves the story that he was FOR us and we got the support we were after. Had we stuck with the story that he had turned AGAINST us, I'm quite sure that he would have continued to resist. When we assumed positive intent, we gave him the space to support us at an even higher level than before. I have often wondered if we had not changed our story and the questions we were asking, would we have been dealing with a Fighting Francis instead of a Provocative Peter?

Asking good questions from a neutral space (versus a self-deprecating or self-important space) allows you to probe the other person's intent before you start making up the wrong stories. Questions are a marvelous tool for assessing the situation.

While questions are very useful in determining true intent, another way to deal with mixed intent is to focus only on the positive side, even when it is not completely evident. In this case, you "turn" a negative statement into a positive statement.

One of the best examples I've experienced in dealing with apparently negative intent occurred with a team I had been working with for years. By this time, I had left banking and started my current business as an executive coach and team facilitator. Assuming positive intent had become a "go-to strategy" that I had been practicing and teaching for years.

In the case of this team, I went into a team retreat with a story in the back of my mind: *"I've been with this team for a long time. I wonder when they will be ready for a facilitator with fresh eyes?"* This mindset contributed to me thinking the worst when one of the team members, Joe, spoke up. While I was describing how the day would go, he said in a frustrated tone: *"Can we just do something different?"*

It hit me in the gut. In essence, he had spoken my own doubts about myself. But that's not what I saw at first. Instead, my eyes saw a full-blown Fighting Francis. I could not believe that this team member was attacking me this way! My first reaction was to defend myself, tell him why he was wrong or further explain why we should keep doing what I had on the schedule. I was almost physically ill.

However, I had been working with this team on how to assume positive intent for a long time. It would have been embarrassing and incongruent to take the bait. So, I sat there with my hand over my mouth to gather myself. After a few deep breaths, and the clear promise to myself to assume positive intent, I found a way. I came back to the team with this statement:

"Can we go back to what Joe said earlier? What will it take for you as a team to have a different conversation in this meeting than the one you typically have?"

The question created a palpable shift in the room. You could almost feel the tension drop. The conversations got deeper. Most importantly, Joe participated as a deeply caring teammate. Provocative Peter had just set up a way for his team to be at their best. His response brought home the power of this practice. I was incredibly grateful to him for setting us up to challenge the norm. The team began to dig into issues that had previously been untouchable. Team members left that day more prepared to address their very significant business challenges.

At dinner that night, I thanked Joe for asking his question. He gave me a funny look, and I briefly wondered why and then forgot it. I left that retreat assuming Joe had truly intended the outcome we had gotten. For years, I would tell that story to other clients as an example for how to assume positive intent.

Several years later, Joe came to my leadership retreat center at Mystic Waters in Western North Carolina for a one-on-one coaching retreat. He was facing a situation where the idea of assuming positive intent would be useful in a particular situation. To illustrate how it worked, I began to give him this very example, forgetting that he was the star of the show. Halfway through the story, I realized that I was telling Joe the story about himself.

Talk about awkward moments! After I caught myself, I

acknowledged that he was part of the story and said, *"I'm going to continue this story and I'm finally going to ask you the question I've wondered about all these years."* At the end of the story I asked, *"What did you really mean that day?"* His response brought home the power of this practice. *"Oh, I was coming after you that day. I was sick of your questions, your techniques, of the whole thing."* Aha! So, he had meant negative intent! Now really curious, I asked: *"Then, what did you think when I turned your comment into a positive question?"* Joe responded, *"I was actually relieved. I didn't have to be the jerk that day."* In other words, Joe might have been a Fighting Francis had I chosen to act defensively instead of assuming positive intent.

My choice set the direction. Joe was BOTH antagonistic and caring that day. By assuming positive intent, we touched only on the caring part, while being aware of his frustration. When we touched the positive, we got more of that. I know from my long experience of focusing on the wrong things that had we touched the negative, we would likely have gotten more of that. Joe's statement would have set the direction that day and the meeting would likely have derailed into a free-for-all.

When I chose to assume positive intent, the focus was channeled into a productive team meeting.

This is exactly the type of situation I feared the most way back when the team wanted to assume positive intent as a core value. My past history had trained me to see only the negative story. Assuming positive intent looked like a road to vulnerability. The safer route seemed to be, "Get them before they get me" or "Head them off at the pass."

Over the years, I've learned that the more I tell myself a story that fits positive intent, the stronger I become and the more likely I am to get a positive outcome. **The strength comes from building the mental tools to resolve problems without getting defensive.**

A Provocative Peter can quickly escalate to a Fighting Francis. You often don't know the difference until you have tested it by assuming positive intent.

Bottom line: Focus on the positive thread of the conversation that supports you – you will get more of what you touch.

CHAPTER SIX

THE ATTACKER: THEY REALLY DO MEAN YOU HARM

"Fighting Francis"

While rare, sometimes the other person simply means to attack you for the sake of derailing you. There are many a Fighting Francis in this world and they usually want to derail you without ever appearing to do anything wrong. Sometimes the attack is sneaky, like a snide remark in the hope that you will respond poorly. Sometimes the attack is more evident. Even in these cases, assuming positive intent is a remarkably effective practice. Nothing bothers your "enemy" as much as you NOT acknowledging their attack. They want to get a rise out of you. That way, they point at your anger and say, "See what a problem you are?" Instead, remain calm and focus on the outcome you want versus. the actions of the attacker. If you take the stance "I will not accept your attack, no matter what you do," you force the person to escalate in order to derail you.

Remember, the practice of assuming positive intent involves getting more of what you touch. If you touch the positive, you tend to get more positive. If you touch the negative, you tend to get more negative. However, despite any assumption of positive intent you offer with Fighting Francis, their return will continue to challenge, undermine, and poke at you. With practiced patience, your positive intent eventually forces the hand of the other person, who will either escalate the negative behavior, or de-escalate to be a Provocative Peter. Every move brings you to another pivotal option. If you continue to choose assuming positive intent, the committed Fighting Francis will be revealed. Their attacks will go from subtle to obvious.

In dealing with a Fighting Francis, we are facing genuine bad behavior. We would be perfectly justified in calling out the snide, the underhanded, and the hateful actions being sent our way. However, playing tit for tat in order to even the score only creates a temporary win for our ego. We have now taken part in the attack. Instead, it's better to assume positive intent as a way to continually redirect the conversation on the positive path you seek. What I'm suggesting in these situations requires extraordinary self-control, compassion, and a good measure of savviness.

This has been especially tough for me to learn. I want Fighting Francis to suffer for being so difficult. After all, he or she is clearly not on my side. Revenge would be nice. But it's also fleeting and doesn't actually work. **Remember that the "opponent" in this circumstance only wins if I accept the attack. This simple knowledge keeps me focused on a bigger picture**.

Assuming positive intent does not excuse the bad behavior, it simply releases you of the responsibility of managing it. It allows you to treat the other person with respect while channeling the focus and efforts to a shared goal. It requires you to be aware of the danger they present without completely focusing on that danger. Otherwise, you will ski into the trees, as I describe in the next section, where I outline some of the principles that will help in navigating the terrain.

Assuming positive intent also holds up a mirror to those multiple facets of our own intentions. We are not blameless in this or any scenario. Remember at the beginning of the book, when I said, "You will also understand that your intentions have multiple facets, some of which are not so friendly and thus may hide from view?" If we are not aware or are unwilling to own our part, our less-than-positive intentions can tend to grab the wheel when we are challenged with a Fighting Francis. Fear has a way of saying, "Here, let me help you out. I'm the only solution to this problem."

When we allow our fears to run us, we shrink our world.

I'm not saying that I succeed every time. To be truthful, far from it. However, when I have been able to walk through the minefield by assuming positive intent at every turn, the outcomes have been extraordinary and even almost miraculous.

One of my clients worked with a board member who had taken up arms against him. In this case, the client was responsible for the financial statements of the organization, and this board member had ferociously questioned the accuracy of the statements in the prior meeting. In preparation for the next meeting, we talked about how to handle the scorching questions that were likely to come. While it seemed counterintuitive and vulnerable to this CFO, he decided to assume positive intent during the meeting. However, it was not as simple as just assuming the positive.

First, we had to address the questions he had about himself. Was he fully confident in the accuracy of the statements? What insecurities was the board member touching? Were there places where he feared that he or his team had missed something?

Addressing these types of internal questions before you're in the line of fire is critical. You only take things personally when they touch on something you judge in yourself. **No one can make you feel judged about something unless you judge yourself about it.**

Once he resolved those questions, he was much less likely to take the attacks personally. Instead, he could focus on what was really happening with the board member. He gained a curious perspective. From that vantage point, he realized it was likely that the board member was paranoid and fearful. Rather than deny or judge the fear, he decided to treat the board member with respect.

In the next meeting, the board member behaved as predicted. The questions were even more scathing than originally anticipated. Fighting Francis was in the room and my client was prepared.

The CFO calmly treated every question as meaningful and

valid. *"I'm so glad you asked that — and we originally had the same question. Here is how we addressed it."* With every calm response, the board member became angrier.

As the attacking-question and reasoned-response cycle continued, it became clear to the rest of the board that the questions were aimed at flustering and discrediting the CFO. Soon, everyone in the room deeply appreciated the CFO's responses and the board member's questions started appearing petty and inappropriate. The meeting ended with the Board supporting the CFO.

As with the story about Joe, there is another chapter in the story.

Within two months, the chairman asked this member to leave the board. The CFO not only stayed, but also advanced in the organization. With this strategy, he provided a role model for his team in how to be strong in the face of attacks from someone in a position of power.

Had the CFO taken the attacks personally and gotten defensive, there is little doubt it would have been him to be let go. This organization had some serious and complicated issues to work through. Because he addressed those issues instead of. worrying about how he looked, the board's confidence in him increased going forward.

When we are under attack — or assume we are — it is a good time to develop true self-awareness. I have found these to be useful questions.

- What is it that I am likely to take personally?

- What do I think I know that may or may not be true?

- What stories am I making up?

- Is there fire where there is smoke? (Are they judging me for something I judge in myself?)

- What do I need to address in myself or in my actions so that I can be clear and honest in this situation?

- Is there something I am hiding that needs to be revealed?

When you answer these questions truthfully, you open a world of possibility to be stronger, less defensive, and more authentic in your relationships. You have room to make mistakes without devastating repercussions. You can focus on solving the problem in front of you instead of trying to look good. You retain the power of choice.

The Fighting Francis situation is by far the most difficult in which to continue to assume positive intent. In this case, they have shown you who they are. As Maya Angelo said, "When someone shows you who they are, believe them." The advice to assume positive intent in this case might seem out of order, but it's not.

There is a difference between assuming positive intent and letting bad behavior off the hook. Assuming positive intent is a safer way to navigate the minefield while addressing bad behavior. When Fighting Francis escalates his or her attack, others will see what's happening, and will often rally to help. The

Fighting Francis characters in this world really do have negative intent. However, when you touch the live wire of the other person's negative intent, you are the one more likely to get scorched. Stay the course and you have a chance to make things right.

Bottom line: When you don't take things personally and you assume positive intent, you force your attackers out of the shadows.

SECTION II

CHAPTER SEVEN
THE PRINCIPLES BEHIND THE PIVOT

These four levels of engagement show a small sampling of the many ways we can feel insulted, undermined, embarrassed, taken advantage of, or judged. The list of ways we can get out of balance with others is truly endless.

However, the choices in how we respond are equally endless. Seeing those choices in the heat of the moment can seem daunting. Even in the simple examples of the one-line emails: *"Can you see me at 3:00 this afternoon?"* Or *"Where is this going?"* there are dozens of choices in what to say — or not say.

Among all those different choices, the first choice is whether to react or respond. We rarely see this choice. To react is automatic. We've been practicing this one for years. We react without thinking. It's reflexive and baked into our repertoire. It happens as sure as we hit the brake when a ball rolls out in front of the car.

Responding is much more difficult. The pivot from reacting to responding requires intention and thought — and practice. It requires us to be in the moment. We must navigate uncomfortable feelings, uncertainty, and the potential for discovering something we may not want to know.

When we react, it's our practiced, automatic patterns going to work for us (or more likely against us). Once we are operating from a pattern, our choices fade into the background. We have a playbook for the situation and perhaps at some level we are feeling threatened. The last thing we want to do is take a moment to get more information or understand another point of view.

On the other hand, if we choose to respond, we must go to work for ourselves. We lose the sense of certainty that we know how this story ends. We must take responsibility for our thoughts and actions. We must risk failure. Instead of relying on a habitual pattern, we have to pause and get curious, which can feel very vulnerable.

Assuming positive intent is a gateway to curiosity, which unlocks the door to a whole different set of possibilities and outcomes. Undoubtedly things might still go poorly. But what if they don't? What if the choice to respond sets you up for more success? What if it offers the other person in the story a gateway to be at their best?

Curiosity allows us to discover what is really going on. We grow when we are curious. We become more capable, aware, and able to solve the problems that really matter. We give our fellow travelers the space and grace to solve the problems with us.

As an adult in the corporate world, it initially seemed to me that curiosity had no place. To me, curiosity was an artifact of childhood. If I were curious, that meant I didn't know what I was doing. My job was to know. Therefore, if I were curious, I wasn't doing my job.

My logic was completely wrong. How did I expect to know the unknowable? As I said at the beginning of this book, the trouble starts when we think we know other people's intentions. We can't possibly know what is going on inside someone else's mind. Moreover, we never know the full picture in any given situation.

Curiosity opens our eyes to seek a more complete picture. Notice I did not say to seek THE complete picture. We will never have that. As leaders, we have to make virtually all of our decisions with incomplete data.

We often make decisions in a sea of complex emotions that often feel more threatening than the risks we are trying to manage. Assuming positive intent is a way of keeping us from making the problems worse than they already are.

Learning to assume positive intent turned out to be a critical pathway to self-awareness for me. By learning to pause before my conditioned pattern kicked in, I became more familiar with what set me off and what rolled off my back. Coming to understand my own patterns for what they were helped me to choose better responses.

With more self-awareness, I had two huge insights.

First, all of my strategies for handling the difficulties that other people presented were nothing more than self-protective armor. My strategies pointed to an absence of inner strength and personal capabilities.

Second, most of the difficulties other people presented were more reflective of their struggles than a signal that they were endangering me.

Leaving the comfort of my old ways of doing things provided the opportunity to learn a whole new skill set. Ironically, these are not the kinds of skills you learn from reading a book. These are more like learning to ride a bike. You find your balance only by hopping on and working through the subtle adjustments required to stay upright.

Assuming positive intent can be surprisingly difficult. The next section takes you through five of the skills—they are more like principles—that helped me along the way.

1. Discern Signal from Noise

2. Focus on What You Want

3. Take Nothing Personally

4. Master Your Stories

5. Develop a Spirit of Inquiry

These five principles apply in many situations. Learning them has helped me in more ways than I can count.

DISCERN SIGNAL FROM NOISE

We live in a world full of noise. There are two primary sources. First, there is external noise. People are vying for our attention every day through the news media, social media channels, advertisements, and more. In our work lives we have a constant stream of meetings, task lists, emails, chats, phone calls, and messages that never stop. We have project deadlines, office politics, customer demands, bosses always asking for more, resource constraints, and more.

Second, there is the internal noise. This is the self-talk, physical sensations, and emotions going on inside of us. Internal noise is especially notable under pressure. Our internal noise informs how we approach what we are doing more than almost anything else.

Here's the key thing to understand about internal noise: it is mostly interference from our past.

Much of our social conditioning has trained us that the feeling of "something being off" is a sign that we have made a mistake. The boss makes a weird expression when you share your work, a colleague sighs when you start talking, or you go into the meeting feeling like you forgot something. Experiencing pressure creates all kinds of physical sensations, from butterflies to a weight on our chest to a feeling of being flushed to that rock in the pit of our gut. Whether it is a signal or noise depends on what we do with it.

That pressure often hits an inner button that sets into motion an established pattern of behavior or response for when we think we've made a mistake. Most often, this is that "perfectionism" button; sometimes it is the "I don't give a shit" button or the "I better start explaining myself button."

In almost every case, our innermost experience is this: we did something wrong. This belief is a leash that ties us to our past.

Suddenly, instead of informing us that we have something we need to pay attention to, our past creates interference, and we start acting like a kid who needs to explain herself to mommy or daddy. Instead of hearing the signal as an opportunity to learn or a situation to address, we think we've made a mistake.

Instead of flowing with the current moment, we beat ourselves up, usually while pretending everything is okay.

The mixed signals create noise in our own internal guidance system and in turn, it sends mixed signals to the people around us.

When I worked for a large bank, hearing people say one thing and mean another was a daily occurrence. We would be in a meeting and someone would be smiling while they said something serious, or they would be scowling and swear that they were not mad. They would say everything was fine while the reports and data said otherwise. It was like living in a fun house with the crazy mirrors creating distortion all over the place.

The result is lack of trust. At first glance, it seems to be a lack of trust in others.

In reality, it's a lack of trust in our **own internal guidance system**.

To true up the signal, we need to recalibrate the system. We do that by changing our interpretation of what that signal means.

After finishing an important team meeting, I faced one of my biggest-ever challenges to assuming positive intent. This meeting had high stakes. It was my first time working with this particular team. The client had put her reputation on the line to call in her colleagues to spend a day focusing on some strategic decisions that her co-workers would have preferred to leave alone.

This team would either leave the meeting with more trust and connection, or they would continue to operate in disconnected silos.

Overall, the meeting went well. The team was highly engaged and had several insights that could only be uncovered when time is dedicated, and space is allowed to explore. As I do with most meetings, we had covered the walls with sticky notes that captured the goals, findings, ideas, and feedback from the meeting.

At the end of the meeting, there was only one sticky note that had a tint of criticism on it. The rest were positive, proactive, and should have filled me with satisfaction for a job well done. Instead, my brain gnawed on the one negative sticky note.

One of the questions I had asked was "What did you want more of? Less of?" The one sticky note stuck out like a glaring spotlight. The client wanted more of something we had not done.

The thoughts came a mile a minute. *"Wait, did we do it and she didn't see it?" "Why does she think that was such a big deal?" "Doesn't she know we didn't have time to do that?" "It's only one comment; maybe she really liked the meeting."* On and on it went, thoughts flooding my senses.

Dammit! The brain that I had been training for years to assume positive intent, to touch the positive, to let the pressure of the situation help me grow and learn—that highly trained brain was letting me down.

Or was it?

My internal guidance system was definitely sending a signal that something was off. I've worked for years to calibrate that system so that I would "know what I know."

At a deeper level than those thoughts, I could feel something was off.

No amount or level of assuming positive intent would override the truth-telling of my guidance system. At that level, I'm trying to tell myself *"You're just making up a story. She loved the meeting."* My guidance system would not let me off the hook with that kind of pat on the head. I knew what I knew. The question was: What would I do with the truth?

As I wrote the report, I marveled at the good work the team had done that day. Step by step, insight by insight, this team solidified their strategy, strengthened their relationships, and finished with a heightened sense of purpose. Every page, every graphic told the story.

But like an unexploded land mine, that one sticky note lurked in the background, waiting to detonate my confidence.

When I reached out via text message for a point of clarification, it was the next day before I got a response. My ego craved an affirmation. My internal guidance system knew it wasn't coming.

The survival mode of my gnawing brain chased the dreaded thoughts: *"I know she was disappointed. This meeting did not meet her expectations. I should have done more. Why did I do the xyz exercise instead of the abc exercise? How did I mess up so badly? She is going to lose respect for me. She will never hire me again. I should not do meetings anymore. I'm not that good at them. I don't like them. I'm never doing this again!"*

Finally, a return text arrived. My first thought: *Please let it sing my praises!* What I wanted it to say: "Lynn, What an amazing experience! So glad we took the risk and did this meeting. Everyone loved it. Thank you. Can't wait to see the report."

What the text actually said: "Lynn, sorry for the delay. Still unpacking our session and it would be too hard to put all my thoughts in text. I'll send you an email and maybe we can have a call next week?" (It would be 5 more days before we could schedule a call. Great. Five more days of wondering, gnawing, and agony.)

No praise—no gushing—and no criticism. However, reading between the lines, my brain gnawed even more. *She knows not to criticize by text. She is trying to figure out how to tell me it wasn't as good as she had hoped.*

The pressure created by this awareness evoked a critical choice point: *Would I react from a proving mindset or respond from an improving mindset? Would I make the elegant pivot?*

What my proving mindset wanted to say: *"What did you think of the meeting? What would you have changed?"* While that sounds pretty neutral, the energy behind it (in my brain at least) was really wanting to send this message: *"Please don't keep me in suspense. I know you didn't like it, so let's just get it over with so I can start defending myself."*

What I actually did was pause, take a deep breath and become aware of all the chatter. I could not fall back on the "you're just making up a story"; my guidance system sent a sharp signal that doing so was the wrong direction to go.

In this case, assuming positive intent involved remembering why we held the working session. Making Lynn feel good—like a Broadway performer getting rave reviews following opening night—was NOT the purpose. My needy ego didn't matter in this case, even though it likes to sit by the table and beg for scraps.

The next (and critical step) in my process of doing team meetings is writing a comprehensive report. My style of report is not minutes, an outline, or a regurgitation of the wall notes. To truly realize the value of the meetings I facilitate, the reports capture the facts, the mood, the insights, and the leadership lessons. More importantly, it's a living document that offers clear steppingstones to the hard work that comes after a day of asking difficult questions.

So HOW I chose to assume positive intent was important. We were not in a conversation about whether the meeting was good or not. The conversation we were in was: "What must happen next for this meeting to be worth the time and attention you invested in it?"

How I answered the next text would either set up the next step for this team or let my fears run the show.

What I wrote was: "Yes, I am actually finishing the first draft right now. We can use the report to get the message you want in front of everyone and I think it would be good to talk about that." And then after several scheduling texts: "My primary intention with the report, besides capturing what we did in the meeting, is highlighting what it will be that you need from your team to be successful. So when you read it, remember that you can add and delete things to get that result."

Now all I had to do was wait five days before we could talk.

Watching my brain was fascinating to say the least. Every

time it strayed into "let's make Lynn feel better" territory, I had to resist the temptation to justify, explain, defend, or even get mad that the expectations were unclear. There was even a point where I caught my brain thinking *She should have said something when we were in the bathroom before we closed the meeting.*

What could have been five days of going into a rabbit hole of "woulda, coulda, shoulda," my thoughts turned into a series of learning moments. Not perfectly—but moving toward proficiency.

On the one hand, I had a picture: Successful meeting, including a report that came to life and recharged this team for the second half of the year.

On the other hand, I had my fear. Or should I say fears. What if I wasn't good enough? What if I made a mistake? What if this client was disappointed? What if I've lost my edge? This list of fears was almost endless.

Both were there and both were true. My choice of where to place my energy and attention would decide what happened next.

If I touched my picture—the team would get a great report and a plan for the rest of the year.

If I touched my fears—we would politely finish the report, the client feels so-so about it, it goes on a shelf, and they end the year in fits and starts with nothing really having changed.

Five days later, when we started the call—after all that time of redirecting my energy to the point of exhaustion—we stayed focused on the desired picture.

I invited questions about the area I suspected had fallen short for her. I could have started by saying, "why didn't you like the xyz?" Or falling on my sword by saying, "I'm so sorry I didn't do that one thing that was on the critical sticky note."

Instead, I framed the questions in a way that invited dialogue. "I know you loved the strategy part of the meeting—and I know you wanted more on the tactics and action plans. What specifically will those things give you?"

Now we were in a problem-solving conversation, not a postmortem. We put our energy on getting her exactly what she needed to finish the year strong, effectively lead her team, and set a high bar with clear accountability hooks.

After we finished, she had two comments. First "This is frickin' awesome," and second, "We totally could not have had this tactical conversation in the meeting. I need to learn to set my expectations at a realistic level."

She also listed a multitude of good things that had already come out of the meeting and the many more she anticipated.

That second comment opened a conversation about everything I've written here. I shared with her my struggle, knowing that the meeting had not met her expectations. After all, we had been working together for years. Assuming positive intent was a frequent topic of our coaching conversations.

With that opening, she affirmed that my "story" was no story. She indeed had left the meeting disappointed and had a similar, agonizing five days.

My internal guidance system had read the situation accurately.

We then went into even more "meta-learning" and talked about how the meeting we were just ending could have gone. I shared with her my gnawing brain, my realization of the different choice points, my fears, and my intention that the whole process would get her the results she was seeking.

Thanks to our mental tools and by sticking with the process, we ended up both relieved and stronger as a result.

The internal signal that once meant "you've made a mistake" instead indicates that you have an opportunity to be curious and to learn. Learning is what drives growth; avoiding mistakes shrinks your world.

Recalibrating the system requires intentionally paying attention to the feeling you get when something is off. Bruce Anderson, founder of Natural Humanship, calls that feeling the "Negative - Positive Pole." It's like a car battery that has energy flow between the negative pole and the positive pole.

That little charge of energy that flows through us can be a signal or it can be noise. When we feel it and react, the negative-positive pole is noise. When we feel it and respond, the pole is a signal.

What I have found for myself is that I spent much of my life trying to shut down the sensation of energy flowing through me that signaled something was off. It seemed wise to ignore it or calm it down or just make it go away. All those strategies just made it worse.

After getting hooked on water skiing in my mid-40s, I started skiing in tournaments. The stakes were low, but the pressure was enormous. Skiing is a single elimination sport. As soon as you quit scoring, your turn is over. Standing on the dock at one of my first tournaments, my arms and legs were like rubber. My heart was pounding. My head was foggy. My negative pole was registering off the charts. I used every meditative technique I had (and I have a bunch) to calm my nerves. And I skied like crap.

I left that tournament wondering where I went wrong. I questioned my ability to calm myself. I questioned the validity of meditation. And I thought something was wrong with me to have let myself feel that way.

A few months later, on a long drive to Florida, I lucked into a random radio conversation with a researcher on performance that seemed to explain it.

Alison Wood Brooks, a Harvard professor, used "ambush karaoke" to first apply pressure to people and then understand the best ways to respond to the pressure. People came into the setting thinking they were going to do one thing. Instead, they discovered that they would be singing to a room full of strangers. Talk about pressure to perform!

She broke the participants into three groups, with a specific instruction on how to deal with their negative pole. Group 1 was to say to themselves "I am calm." Group 2 was to say, "I am anxious." Group 3 was to say, "I am excited."

Then she had them sing and rated them on pitch, volume, and rhythm. The rating was scored on a percentage scale. Here's how the different people scored under pressure:

Group 1 - *I am calm*: 53%

Group 2 - *I am anxious*: 69%

Group 3 - *I am excited*: 81%

These findings were both stunning and inspiring for me.

It seems that trying to calm myself just provoked more nervousness. Telling myself I *should* be able to perform because I *should* be able to calm myself knocked my mind out of alignment with my body.

What the researcher found was this: When we go against what our body already knows—that it is time to rise to the occasion—we set up an unresolvable conflict. Allowing the feelings to exist—and calling them excitement—frames the bodily hullabaloo as a productive source of energy.

And guess what? It works. On the very trip where I learned about this research, I stood on the starting dock feeling great pressure. I had not skied in months and I was surrounded by many of the highest performers in the sport. It was like being at a tournament.

The nonsense in my body started knocking me around as I buckled my boot. I unconsciously said out loud, "I'm so nervous." Then I caught myself, and happily shouted at my driver, "I'm so excited!" For the first time in memory under those conditions, I ran that first pass off the dock and had a great set.

The science of top performance has been around for a long time. Top-level performers in all fields have found a way to use their nerves to their advantage. That is why they win.

We get to choose how we frame the signals we receive. When our negative pole goes up, we can either react automatically or we can respond, which requires intention, thought, and work.

The feeling we get is a true signal. The noise happens when we misinterpret the signal. When we ignore it or go into our past to interpret the feeling as an indication that we need to beat ourselves up or reach for our defensive weapons (i.e., justifying, explaining, capitulating, judging, etc.), we have made a choice to react. It's so automatic that it doesn't feel like a choice.

Assuming positive intent acts as a sort of pause button, giving us a moment to read the signal before we react out of habit. It prevents the noise of our past from interfering with the situation that is happening right now.

If you must jump into the head of the other person, assuming positive intent puts you in the shallow water where you can still breathe.

It's incredibly useful to make the distinction between thinking you know someone else's intentions and reading the signals that come through your internal guidance system.

Speaking with one of my clients who was navigating a difficult challenge at work, she said "Lynn, he's just not a good person" referring to one of the colleagues with which she needed to work. These were senior level executives in a very large organization. She had gotten signals that he was neither supportive nor honest. Unfortunately, his undermining behavior was discreet. He had a way of making himself look good while subtly putting others down. She was mystified that his boss and others had not picked up on his untrustworthiness. It was as clear as day to her.

His behavior continually made it more and more difficult for her to get her job done well. She found herself second-guessing her early impressions of him and at the same time fearing that he was making undercutting moves that could eventually come back to bite her.

She was torn between an inner knowing that she could not trust this colleague and an awareness that she had little or no visible evidence on which to act. She wanted to assume positive intent, but she could not get past the signal that he was untrustworthy.

I have found this to be true more times that I can count. There are two parts to the dilemma. The first is the accuracy in reading the signal. The second is navigating the situation.

Our internal guidance system lets us know when something

is off. It's what we do with the signal that either helps or hinders us.

In this case, her awareness led her to judge her colleague. "He's not a good person." There was a part of her that was angry with him; after all, who was he to make working with him so difficult? How dare he! Being on guard took a lot of energy and caused her more than one night of lost sleep.

Her awareness, coupled with her judgment of him, set up the conditions for her to treat him with caution. Her judgment and anger sent a signal to him as well. He went into his own noise about her. As they continued to work together, the cycle of mistrust escalated.

She really did not want to assume positive intent in dealing with him. To some extent, it felt like giving him a "get out of jail free" card. In her deepest knowing, she knew he was self-serving and untrustworthy. Assuming positive intent was just not fair. She would rather he be punished.

Once she reached this insight, she began to see the folly of her dreams of justice. People behave badly. People have self-serving intentions. People can be difficult. Especially at her level in the executive suite, there would be no arbiter to take her side and trade her colleague out in favor of a better person.

She also began to learn it was she who would set the conditions for the story to end differently. Even though her reading of the situation was likely accurate, assuming positive intent guided her navigation of the situation. While it was never as clean as a flip of a switch, the relationship improved as she began to focus on the problems they were solving together, rather than on the behavior that felt so personal.

When I first learned to assume positive intent, it was these types of situations that presented true harm that most concerned — and confused — me. Why would I make myself even more vulnerable than I already am?

With lots of practice and more than a few errors and miscalculations, it became evident to me that assuming positive intent kept me on the high road. It kept me from being an unwitting player in the other person's game.

One such event happened to me in the subway system of the Washington DC Metro years ago.

As I was coming down the escalator with my suitcase in tow, I casually looked at the crowd preparing to board a train leaving the station. Of the hundreds of people milling in the area, for some reason, one man drew my attention. He was in the group to my left about to get on the outgoing train. He appeared to be looking for someone rather than making a move for the train. It was a fleeting moment and then I started looking for my destination on the far right.

My path was taking me up the next escalator to the retail area which also housed my hotel for the evening. Suddenly, the same man who was in line to leave on a train was one step below me on the escalator — way too close for my comfort.

In an instant, I had a flood of thoughts. *What is he doing here? Did he change his destination? Why is he standing so close to me?* My immediate choice was to ignore him. He had other plans.

He said something—I can't remember exactly what—and I gave him my best "traveler's polite reply" indicating I was not interested in further conversation. I looked the other way to reinforce my message. He failed to take the hint and asked another question. This one really got my attention; it was something along the lines of, "Where do you live?"

I tried another quick, vague answer followed by another disinterested look the other way. No luck. His next question was, "Are you here on business?"

At this point, his behavior struck me as extremely odd. He was acting overly familiar. This was not the normal social banter of fellow travelers. If only it could be over! But we were only halfway up this very long escalator. Plus, I distinctly remembered he was preparing to board a train going the other way just moments before.

With my senses on high alert, I decided to take a different approach. I did my best to strike a neutral tone. "Why do you ask?"

He looked shocked and said, "Hey, I'm just trying to be friendly."

There was something about his expression that did not read

so innocently. As the escalator continued its excruciatingly slow progress, I became grateful that my question had bought me some time. If I were not able to get this guy to leave me alone on the escalator, he would be even more difficult to shake when I was going to my hotel. Which was the last place I wanted him. Now I just needed to say something that would put an end to this conversation and keep him from trailing me. I decided not to go straight to my hotel. Instead, I planned to head toward the security station for the retail area.

Even though he had not directly threatened me, I was feeling threatened. By now, I had seen enough Fighting Francis types to know that I could make it worse. And there was a tiny chance he really was just trying to be friendly. I decided to assume positive intent while making it clear I was not playing along with whatever game he was playing. "Thank you. I'm surprised you picked me out of the crowd. What are you trying to gain in having this conversation?"

He looked shocked and then said something that indicated I was taking this the wrong way. I said something like, "I probably am, but I'm not in the habit of making friends on crowded escalators." Again, I did my best to say it with a neutral tone and without accusation.

By now we were at the top of the escalator. I was curious if he would continue to a destination up here or try to follow me. As I set my sights on the security station, I kept this guy in my peripheral vision.

As soon as he reached the top of the escalator, he made a U-turn and went back down. With great relief, I went on to my hotel.

Sometimes people really do mean you harm. I will never know what this guy was up to that day. When I curiously asked why he was having this conversation, I threw him off his game without directly calling him out. I don't know what would have happened if I had gotten stuck trying to be polite or if I had directly accused him. Would he have tried to keep asking me questions once we got off the escalator? Would he have followed me, or even worse, tried to grab me or grab my bag or something else? I will never know. What I do know is that if he were the innocent traveler just making conversation on the escalator, he would not have gone back down into the subway station. He would have gone on to his destination on the upper level.

My internal guidance system gave me an accurate reading that day. Assuming positive intent kept me from activating the potential negative intent this guy might have had.

CHAPTER NINE

FOCUS ON WHAT YOU WANT

One of our natural human tendencies is to focus on the thing that seems to present the strongest threat. It's part of our human Survival Mode. When dealing with the electricity of someone else's intention, we need to recognize a critical principle: You get more of what you touch.

Another way of saying it is that your energy will follow your attention. As you saw earlier in the book, I trained my attention to find the negative at every turn. Being able to pick apart an argument, watch for the way someone would burn me, and live behind a self-protective wall of assuming negative intent caused me more problems than it solved. Why? Because I spent so much time touching the very thing I didn't want.

One of my friends had a favorite saying that he would use on me extensively: "Chill out." There is one thing I can tell you about that saying, not only for me, but for anyone ever in need of chilling out. Telling a person who needs to chill out—and I definitely was in that category—to chill out will get you exactly the opposite outcome. Focusing on the problem actually magnifies the problem.

My friend would say "Chill out," which put me in touch with

the slightly panicked, very nervous side of myself. It was as if an electrical charge ran through me. Whatever nervousness, tension, and fear that was running through me that prompted him to tell me to calm down suddenly multiplied ten-fold. Now I directed my wrath at him. His hands would go up and he would say something like "See? You really need to chill." Yes. I. Did.

When we try to fix a problem like having a friend that needs to chill, or wanting the respect of our peers, or wondering if we can really trust our co-workers, touching the problem only makes it worse.

It's important to learn how and on what to direct our focus. I learned to snow ski late in life. Already tall and having experienced a fall from my fully developed height, I was a cautious skier from the start. Nonetheless, I looked at some of the more advanced skiers with envy. Seeing skiers take on steep, bumpy slopes inspired me to keep getting better.

One day, my ski buddies and I decided to go on a slope with a big tree in the middle of it. Suddenly, all the wide-open space I had been using to get myself down the mountain felt like it had been cut in half. The first time down the slope, my legs were shaking and all I could think about was the tree, which seemed to take up the entire slope. Try as I might to avoid it, I skied right to that tree. I didn't crash into it, but the tree was like a magnet that drew me to it. After I stopped and gathered myself, as I skied away, I resolved to miss it the next time.

We got on the chair lift and I headed back to the "tree slope," fully committed to do better this time. Standing at the top of the slope, the tree loomed larger than ever. That was the thing I would avoid. In my mind it sounded like this: AVOID THE TREE. In other words, it was very loud and in keeping with my commitment to really, really avoid the tree this time.

Turn by turn, as I went down the slope, I kept my focus solidly on avoiding that tree. Never have I been so committed to avoiding something. As I made my way down, I was also jealously aware of the people smoothly skiing past me and the tree. What did they have that I didn't? Before I knew it, I was back to my starting place. I had skied straight to the tree. Again, I stopped myself before hitting it.

Focusing on the problem had only made it worse.

It would take a few more times before I tried something different. One of my ski buddies said something like, "Quit focusing on the tree." To my ears, it sounded like "Chill out." But maybe he had a point.

The next time down, I shifted my focus to the white space between the tree and the edge of the slope. Turn by turn, my picture of getting down the slope was framed by the tree and the edge of the slope. Before I knew it, I had skied by the tree and continued a fluid run to the bottom of the hill.

So that was it. Focusing on the picture I wanted instead of focusing on what I did not want changed the outcome. Skiing to the white space did the trick.

Assuming positive intent allows us to ski to the open white space on the slope. We touch what is coming at us with the picture in mind of what we want instead of what we don't want.

Looking at the "Provocative Peter" story of Joe, he was presenting two streams of "electricity" in the team meeting that day. The bigger stream was his frustration and anger with the situation, with his team, and with me. There was also a tiny stream of deep caring and wanting this team to do their best work together.

It was so tempting for me to try to stop him from being angry and frustrated with his team and especially with me. Besides feeling slightly betrayed, I was also fearful of being exposed as not being up for the task. Calling him out felt like a very justified reaction to his comment.

Had I touched that stream of electricity, I would have gotten more of what I didn't want. He and I both would have been virtually "electrocuted", and we would have had a vastly different outcome.

I know this because more times than I can count, I focused on the anger or self-interest or untrustworthiness of another person. This approach almost always ended up causing me more harm than the other person. No matter how justified it seemed to call them out for their egregious behavior, somehow, I was the one who got burned.

This is true whether handling a short-term situation, like the many grocery store clerks I berated for mismanaging my groceries, or a long-term resentment I carried from a since forgotten misdeed. It was as if I swallowed the poison and hoped the other person died. It only makes things worse for me.

In the story of Gary demanding that our team explain why we were late coming back from breakfast, the more my team members explained to him why we were late, the more irate and empowered he became. As every person went around the room touching his anger, it was as if power went from the explainer to the demander.

Amy broke the current of electricity by asking a different question. Her even, neutral, curious way of speaking carried no judgment. It was like she was aware of the anger, but she chose to touch something else.

Like all of us, Amy was aware of the "tree in the middle of the slope." Yet while the rest of us focused on what we didn't want or like, she chose to focus on the white space, fully aware that the situation was framed by Gary's anger. She focused on what she wanted, and she got more of that.

The next time you are facing a Provocative Peter or Fighting Francis, test yourself. See if you can see through the crackling electricity of what you don't want into the small, tiny kernel of goodness that will bring the best out of that other person. If you can't find it—and it's difficult when strong emotions or untrustworthy behavior leads the way—make it up. Assume it. Touch what you want. Stay with it, without judgment or fear.

More than once, I've received an email from a colleague,

when my first response was something along the lines of "What a stupid idea!" or "Did he even read the email?" or "She doesn't have a clue!" That's become my signal to slow down, breathe, and recognize my own judgment and fear. Then I pull out a pocket question, which helps me make the pivot to a more productive mindset. "How did you arrive at this viewpoint?" or "Do you have data I haven't considered?" or "Can you take me through your thinking?"

A lot of times, when people hear me give this recommendation, they think it means to ignore unacceptable behavior. That is NOT what I'm saying. Just as with the tree in the middle of the ski slope, I ignore such a thing at my peril. There is a difference between awareness and focus. You need to be aware of the other person's behavior while at the same time recognizing that you cannot actually know the full portfolio of their intentions.

Ascribing an intention to behavior is where it can backfire on you. Assuming positive intent keeps you from overlaying your belief about why someone behaved the way they did.

I cannot recall a time when I genuinely followed this principle when the outcome didn't open my eyes to understanding the situation at a deeper level. However, there have been many times when I just couldn't get myself there. It was not because the other person was just so worthy of assuming negative intent. It was because I took it so personally.

CHAPTER TEN
TAKE NOTHING PERSONALLY

Here's the greatest discovery I've had on this ongoing journey to assume positive intent: when I can't assume positive intent in a situation — no matter how hard I try — it's all about me.

My tunnel vision comes from something I'm not willing to face in myself. It could be that I have a question about whether I'm adding value. It might be a sense of guilt about not having done something I should have. My confidence in a certain area might be low.

When someone touches one of those "soft spots," my defenses go up and my automatic thinking takes over. "They must be the bad guy here." I think and operate accordingly.

My automatic thinking comes from a belief that they are doing something TO ME. Because I'm hurt or surprised or scared or feeling bad, I don't see it as a belief but rather as absolute truth.

If you choose to operate from the belief that it is NEVER personal, you effectively disarm even the most vicious attack. This belief becomes reality because you make it so.

There is a secret to believing that it is never personal, and it is this: When you make something personal, it's because it IS personal. The thing you are taking personally is pointing to doubt you have about yourself. There is good news in this: if you learn to pay attention, you can deal with your self-doubts in a constructive way that makes you stronger. If you keep taking things personally, you may feel vindicated, but you won't grow in self-awareness or strength.

When you choose to assume positive intent vs. taking things personally, you avoid taking in the negative because your focus is on the positive. It doesn't mean the negative isn't there—it just means that you choose not to engage with it. And when you don't engage with it, you are freed up to focus on what you want to have happen.

My taking things personally caused a small disagreement to turn into a big thing with a close colleague. When he was making a major decision about where to place responsibility for the management of significant assets, he said he did not trust my team to handle it. As he was talking things through, he made several critical remarks about my team that did not appear relevant to the decision. I took his comments personally and the conversation went into a deep, dark hole. I told myself a story that he was being egotistical and arrogant. I thought he was trying to make me look bad and keep me in my place. I got angry and defensive and attacked him back—all the while feeling justified in my thinking that he was the "bad guy" here. The conversations got heated and occasionally, even loud.

Not until we were deep into the disagreement days later (at a point where I realized that this thing could seriously damage our relationship) did I consider asking a question about from where his point of view was really coming. When I was able to get grounded and ask some better questions — with help from another colleague — a different picture began to emerge.

With some guidance, I could see that my colleague had a point.

When I took his criticism personally instead of getting curious enough to ask what he was trying to achieve, I turned the conversation into a posturing moment rather than a moment of clarity. It almost cost me the relationship. Once we focused on the deeper questions, he realized that while he had the right inclination about the decision, unjustifiably attacking my team would actually keep him from implementing the better choice.

As we debriefed the whole situation, he came back later and apologized about his comments about my team. It was never personal.

When I did my own self-examination about why I made it personal, I realized that he was touching on some questions about my team (and my leadership of the team) that I had not been willing to face. His actions simply triggered a doubt that I was already carrying. I was later grateful for the insight, as I was able to own my mistakes in leadership while at the same time realizing that those mistakes did not make me unworthy.

My own work in learning to assume positive intent is to make it a practice to not take things personally BEFORE the situation becomes difficult or even precarious. It truly amazes me the power we have to navigate through sticky situations when we have that internal sense of confidence and strength to face our doubts and questions about ourselves.

Here's the key: the assumption you make, or the story you tell yourself about why someone else is doing something becomes the script from which you will operate. You are the co-writer of the story. It is your response, not the other person's action that decides how the chapter ends.

EXAMPLE	YOUR REACTION	ASSUMING POSITIVE INTENT
No feedback	He's ignoring me She doesn't want to deal with it	He's busy – I'll remind him My email might be in spam. I'll phone him
Feedback suggesting a different way	He's trying to control me. She doesn't think I'm any good	I have a chance to do better She cares enough to give feedback
Negative feedback	He doesn't think I know what I'm doing	Tell me how I can improve

You may be wondering how to avoid taking things personally when it *feels* so personal? The key is giving yourself some distance, stepping back to see the situation as a whole.

There are several levels of "stepping back." As a starting point, learn to view the situation as the "story watcher," as if you are watching it on a large screen. Oh, how I wish I could always do this! If you succeed one in ten times, it will make things better for you. And even when you are deep into a situation where you are taking it personally, you can recover if you will just remember to stay above the fray.

Tips for Staying Above the Fray

- Listen for the undercurrents in the plot

- Instead of considering comments and questions as directed at you, ask yourself what is driving the other person to say or ask these things

- Recognize that their actions say more about them than about you

- Commit to tease out the story behind the story

- Rather than judge, get curious

- Rather than fight, be interested

- Rather than disconnect, be caring

- Rather than saying this is wrong, explore the consequences and fallout

As you get more comfortable with staying above the fray, you will find there is another level of taking nothing personally. Eventually, you will learn to separate your actions from your true self-worth. This is the ultimate level of "stepping back." Becoming deeply grounded in who you are at your core is deep work and it takes a lifetime of practice. You learn to allow people to say something about your ability to do a skill; allow no one the right to say anything about **who you are**. We take things personally when we confuse a statement about our actions with a statement about our worthiness.

This lesson truly hit home for me when I decided to learn to drive a boat for tournament slalom skiers. I asked a top driver to coach and mentor me. His first statement was, "Are you sure? You have to have thick skin to learn to do this. Just because you can already drive a boat doesn't mean you can drive at this level." My answer to him was this: "Nothing you tell me about how to drive a boat will say anything about who I am. Bring it on." Little did I know what I was asking for! Over the next several years, we worked together, with increasingly more difficult situations for me to practice.

My mentor was demanding. He would say something that might seem nitpicky. There were times it felt personal. More than once he was hard on me. Most of the time, I said to myself, "This will make me a better driver." And it has, even though I frequently told myself an unproductive story that looked like this: *"He will never trust me, I'm doing what he told me."* or *"Why can't he see how good I am?"* Most of the time I caught myself and listened to his guidance. If I had stuck with taking things personally, I'm quite sure that my lessons and growth would have ended.

When we take things personally, we stop our learning and perhaps forfeit a good outcome. We start defending instead of listening. We get hurt instead of hearing. We focus on offloading pain more than getting better. We feed our ego instead of feeding our higher self. We often do not realize how much we have our self-worth wrapped up in our work identity.

We take things personally out of habit, because of our internal questions about ourselves or as a defense. Choosing to do so is like taking a pill that saps our strength. We take in the "bad stuff" in order to protect ourselves and it actually makes us more vulnerable.

More often than not, the other person does not mean to make it personal. Sometimes they do. We don't have to be naïve about this. Just because someone intends to makes something personal does not mean you have to take it personally. If you stay grounded and clear, you can see through their actions and give them a chance to take the higher road. As Josh Waitzkin said in *The Art of Learning*, "If aggression meets empty space it tends to defeat itself."

Try it for a while and see what happens for you. Commit to take nothing personally. Get curious instead. Ask really good questions. When you take something personally (and trust me, you will take something personally!), pay attention to the story you make up about why it happened.

MASTER YOUR STORIES

I ended my TEDx talk with this sentence: "You can become the co-writer of an entirely new story for your life." If you are looking for a new source of power in your life, look no further than the truth of this sentence. Now for the difficult part: implementing it in your daily life.

Master your stories and you virtually remove the ability of others to get to you. Notice, I said "your stories," not "the story." Mastering your stories is super challenging. Most of the time our story is invisible to us, hidden in the background and informing what we see, hear, and feel. We don't realize that we are telling ourselves a story about a situation. We just assume that we see the whole truth and nothing but the truth, when in reality, we have just a few scattered data points.

Our stories determine how we act in any given situation. Because our stories are so automatic, we rarely notice that they are stories instead of facts. Our story is certainly not "the story."

Those stories create a cascading effect. When you choose negative stories, filled with inferences about how someone is mistreating you or disrespecting you, or how your employees don't know what they are doing or how the board member is out to get you, you set certain things in motion.

These kinds of scenarios play out every day in business:

- You've told that manager seven times to reorganize his department in preparation for the huge changes coming and it's still not done. He's disrespectful and just doesn't get it.

- The boss failed to include you in the latest board meeting. She must be sending you a message or has lost confidence in your ability to present at a high level.

- One of your peers is contradicting everything you say in the monthly review meeting. He is clearly trying to get all the credit and undermine you.

Notice how quickly we see a situation and decide what it means. We see a behavior, an expression, some body language and we quickly fill in the blanks with a story. We have minimal data points and suddenly we somehow KNOW what is going on. We believe our story as if it were handed to us in a certified document with the "truth seal of approval." We just don't realize that it's a STORY, made up by our minds to solve discordance and discomfort. We just move on.

Epictetus, the Roman philosopher, said: "He was sent to prison. But the observation 'he has suffered evil,' is an addition coming from you."

The "addition coming from you" refers to the stories we tell about why things happen.

Our stories are fertile ground for learning about ourselves and they are the pivot point for assuming positive intent. Any intent that we assume about another person's actions is based on a story that we are making up. We simply cannot know all the facts. And as you saw in Chapter 6, even a Fighting Francis can be disarmed by sticking with the facts and not adding fuel to the fire.

Have you ever had someone not answer an email and you start telling yourself stories about why that is?

"He is upset because I got the promotion and he didn't."

"She doesn't want to do the work I asked."

"She doesn't want to talk about this sticky subject."

The stories are endless and chances are that your email is in the other person's spam box. However, if you stick to the story that makes them a villain and you a victim, you have injected an element into the relationship that can cause damage. Your resentment might just show up next time you meet in the hallway or at a critical meeting.

Why is all of this so important? Your stories are a window into YOUR internal operating rules and beliefs. They reflect a compilation of your victories and defeats, your happy moments and your despair. They also create the roadmap for how you write the story for your life, and when you couple the tendency of the survival brain to see the worst in everything, your hidden stories create negative outcomes.

I've hurt myself more times than I can count by telling the

wrong story.

I had a simple, funny and embarrassing incident recently with my husband and a bottle of soy sauce. He brought home some chicken fried rice from his favorite Chinese restaurant. The day he brought it home, he made a point of asking if we had soy sauce as he opened the refrigerator looking for it. Before I could answer, he held up a full bottle and said, "Never mind – we have a brand-new bottle." Strike that one from the grocery list. I thought, *If I decide to make the dish needing a soy sauce marinade later in the week, we are covered.*

The next morning, he had finished his breakfast before I came into the kitchen. The first thing I noticed on the counter was an empty bottle of soy sauce. Now, let me tell you — I don't think of soy sauce as a condiment for anything involving breakfast. So, I had to ask, "What happened to all the soy sauce?" My incredulousness touched his impish button, so with a twinkle in his eye, he said, "I used it all."

Now my crazy self-talk started. I was thinking *How could he have used a whole bottle? What is he cooking that might need a WHOLE BOTTLE of soy sauce? What about me – what if I need soy sauce? How am I going to make my dish? He is making more work for me. Is he trying to be wasteful on purpose?* These thoughts came one after the other at a speed that would get me arrested.

The stories I started making up were epic. One involved my husband suddenly deciding to cook and something delicious was marinating in the fridge as we spoke. Another involved him emptying the bottle into another container just so he could mess with me. The most ridiculous involved him actually using the whole bottle on a single serving of rice. The more stories I made up the more my mind closed in on finding an explanation for how a full bottle of soy sauce was now empty.

I wish I could tell you how funny this all was—but I can't. I actually got quite annoyed when he refused to explain the empty bottle to me. My wise husband stopped the nonsense by opening the door and pulling out the still full bottle of soy sauce. "I found another one that was almost empty and decided to use that one first. You leapt."

What a simple explanation! It never occurred to me that this might be a different bottle. Now I felt relieved and embarrassed. Relieved that there was a good explanation and embarrassed because I let my mind run away with making up stories. Again. I leapt.

The stories we make up are a significant barrier to assuming positive intent. Our minds love to find a reason for things. In the absence of a full explanation, we will fill in the blanks and don't even realize we are doing it.

Artists use this tendency to leave something to the imagination in their work, knowing that the brain will fill in details, often in a way that is pleasing to the viewer. Writers do the same—often the passages that set up a gripping scene and stop short of giving every detail are the ones that we enjoy the most.

We have the same power to generate more empowering stories in our day-to-day lives. However, our survival brain, personal history, and context tend to send our stories in the "OMG, I'm about to get screwed!" direction. Because it happens so fast and is so reflexive, we take those stories for truth. We often don't consider that something else might be going on.

Understanding the stories we make up is incredibly fertile ground for developing deep self-awareness—transformative awareness of our own personal patterns, habits, and operating rules. These patterns, habits, and rules operate in the background, taking over our decisions. Your mind is lovingly offering you an "easy button" to create shortcuts that make your thinking automatic. Ever feel like you just keep doing the same thing over and over again? That's your background operating system at work, making life "easy" for you. The stories you make up are not based on the facts of the situation. They are based on your personal filters much more than on what is really happening.

I will say this: I find it really hard work—hard personal work—to make up a better story. With the help of my coaches over the years, I've learned more about myself by learning to assume positive intent than almost any other practice that I have implemented. (Meditation is another regular practice I have found extremely useful.)

In some ways, it's more fun to act on those negative stories, filled with ill-informed assumptions about how others feel and think. More often than I can count, I have set off a cascade of unwanted consequences, which predictably enough, actually magnified the negative stories.

When you watch my TEDx talk, you will hear tales of the ways those other stories negatively impacted me in my career, sidelined my goals, isolated me from others, and left me feeling pretty angry at myself and the world around me. My negative stories caused me to co-write a story for my life that did not work very well at all.

Alternatively, when you assume positive intent, you set a completely different set of cascading possibilities into motion. When you become aware of the stories you tell yourself, and decide to change those stories, you inspire a new direction for your life and create true strength in yourself.

You do not have to tell the stories that you have been telling — you can change the stories.

Assuming positive intent is that simple, pivotal action that empowers you to become aware of your own motivations, hurts, patterns, and operating rules. When you can't assume positive intent by telling a better story, it's because of something operating in you that is NOT YOU. It's an old story that you adopted. It can be changed.

All it takes is to practice, practice, and practice some more. When you get stuck, ask for help. Learning to tell a new story has changed the trajectory of my life. It can change yours too.

Chapter Twelve
DEVELOP A SPIRIT OF INQUIRY

Much of the work of assuming positive intent is internal. We start making choices from the moment we get the first signal. In the best case scenario, we react and then catch ourselves and respond instead. In the worst case, we react and do the same thing we've always done.

It's what we do in that "catch and respond" moment that informs our actions and allows us to discern the signal, focus on what we want, take nothing personally, and pen better stories.

The sequence for me goes something like this:

Pause - Assume Positive Intent - Get Curious - Ask a Question

The first three steps are internal. They are the "catch" that gets me ready for the pivot. Once I've gone through those steps, it's time to "respond." Start with a question or two. Rather than leaping to a conclusion, take a step back and gather more information.

In almost every story where assuming positive intent made the difference, the pivot happened around a question.

Remember Jerry, who was upset about the email that said: "Can you come see me at 3:00?" The question that pulled him out of his story was: *"What other possible stories would explain this email?"*

In the case of Gary, who was so mad at our group for being late from breakfast, the question that Amy posed that broke through was, *"What are you trying to accomplish here?"*

With a question like that, tone matters. Amy asked the question with a spirit of inquiry and curiosity. Had she asked it with a defiant or angry tone, it would have set in motion a whole different set of actions.

The question that turned Mark, the executive sponsor who suddenly was not supporting us anymore, was, *"What would you like for us to do to keep you more in the loop?"*

With Joe, who started the team meeting by asking, "Can we just do something different?" the pivotal question ended up being a variation of his question, *"What will it take for you as a team to have a different conversation in this meeting than the one you typically have?"*

Asking a question gives us another moment to pause and gather ourselves to respond rather than react. It also gives our brain a challenge to come up with a good question, rather than falling into the trap of thinking it knows what is happening.

At moments when the pressure is high and our negative pole is up, it can be difficult to strike a neutral tone. That's why the sequence has a step to "Get Curious" before asking the question. In that moment, you actually allow the other person to inform your actions.

114

With curiosity, you can follow their lead in a way, which actually keeps you in the lead. Why? Because you are crafting good questions that are worth exploring.

When I was learning to facilitate learning programs, it was very different than lecturing. In facilitation, my job was to ask provocative questions that the people in the room could consider and learn by solving the problems presented.

Most of the time, we were leading change with new ways of doing things. People were resistant. If I had my way, everyone would just go along and do what they were supposed to do.

Instead, they pushed back, criticized the decisions, and often said "that won't work." My reflexive response was "yes it will." Once we got into that kind of back and forth, it was like a game of tug of war that nobody could win.

When you are playing tug of war, forward motion is almost impossible. It's hard to get any traction at all. Yet my job as the facilitator was to help people solve problems, not be more resistant. Setting up this kind of impasse just made things worse.

I could not see a way out. One of my facilitator coaches gave me the idea of having a prepared question when the inevitable push back came. So many came into the meeting with the thought, "I know how this movie ends; I've seen it a thousand times." When someone in the room said any variation of "That won't work," my new response should be, "What would work?"

Again, tone is important. If that question is delivered with defiance, the tug of war escalates. When that question is delivered with curiosity, a real conversation can happen.

Here are some questions that you can ask someone who is acting in inexplicable ways:

- Could you take me through your thinking about how you reached that decision?

- I feel like I am missing some key information here. What are you seeing that I might not?

- What alternatives did you consider before coming to this decision?

I think of questions like this as "pocket questions." When we are under pressure, it can be difficult to come up with a great question. For me, it was helpful to be able to pull the question out of my pocket and use it at critical moments.

We can also ask ourselves questions, especially when we are in situations that are more protracted and happening over time. In the Fighting Francis case, when the board member had taken up arms against the CFO, we went through several critical questions. Once he addressed these honestly, he was much more prepared to navigate the situation:

- What is it that I am likely to take personally?

- What do I think I know that may or may not be true? What stories am I making up?

- Is there fire where there is smoke? (Are they judging me for something I judge in myself?)

- What do I need to address in myself or in my actions so that I can be clear and honest in this situation?

- Is there something I am hiding that needs to be revealed?

These questions require a level of self-awareness, which is a foundational pillar of leadership. As I shared in so many of my stories, a lack of self-awareness caused me to be defensive and judgmental as a form of self-protection.

When I was able to address my own self-doubts and insecurities, it became much easier for me to assume positive intent on the part of someone else. I could give them the grace that I had learned to give myself.

Truthfully, most of the time, it was a misinterpretation on my part. I was creating my own self-fulfilling prophecies by focusing only on the negative in so many situations. I tended to touch the live wire by thinking I knew their intentions.

We can't possibly know what is happening in the inner world of other people. We can only see what we see. When we develop a spirit of inquiry and use questions as our steppingstones to understanding, we deepen our relationships and avoid the misunderstandings that lead to unproductive conflict.

Great questions allow us to tune into the signal that is coming through the noise. They help us master our stories.

There is one question that helps more than any other when I see someone behaving in inexplicable ways: **"What would explain this behavior that also fits the facts of the situation?"**

Make a note of that question, highlight it, write it down. Because that question will help you make up a better story on which to act and can set things off in a much more productive direction.

CONCLUSION
WORTH THE RISK

Taking offense was once a form of personal armor for me. It gave me the illusion of control, as if seeing the other person's intention to harm me could actually protect me from them. Never did I realize that I might be misreading the situation. Never did I consider that the other person might be wearing their own armor. Never did I consider how my armor might signal they should be watching out for me. Nope — I just put on the highly conductive metal suit and touched the electricity of their cautious intention. Ouch. All I did was show them that they needed to watch out for me.

Instead, I could have been calling out their best intentions.

Learning to assume positive intent as a regular practice did not happen overnight. Remember my reluctance at the beginning of this book? I'm still learning it. I still fail at times.

Once in a while, I remember to assume positive intent just in the nick of time. My TEDx talk was sparked from a moment of assuming positive intent, right after I had taken offense at the woman who would ultimately become my TEDx speaking coach. I was parking for a charity event at a house in a neighborhood, and as I got out of my car, the woman who had just parked in front of me said, *"I think you have parked too close to my car. I won't be able to get out."* She was not smiling or friendly — she had that neutral face. My first reaction, after all these years, was still to say, "How dare she?"

It was so tempting to start justifying or to get angry. To gather myself, I gave myself a moment to make sure my bumper was not ON her car. I took a breath and focused on what I wanted. Since we were both going to the same party, I wanted to start things off on the right foot. Then I said, "I think they need us to park close so that we can fit a lot of cars in here. If you need to leave before the event is over, come find me and I will move my car." The tension was broken, and we walked into the event together.

Later in the evening, she mentioned that she was one of the organizers of the upcoming TEDxTryon event and that she had heard from some of the people at the event that I was a speaker and that I coached leaders. Through our conversations at the event we made a genuine connection. Internally, I was so grateful that I had not been bitchy with her during the earlier car incident. Eventually she asked if I would be interested in applying to speak at TEDxTryon, and if so, what the topic would be.

Here's where it gets interesting: I was aware of the event and had made a deliberate choice NOT to apply. I love working with live audiences, but I prefer a much more interactive format than the TED stage offers. I said to her, *"TED is not for me. Give me a topic, a microphone, and an audience and I can keep them engaged for*

10 minutes." She laughed and let me know in no uncertain terms that a TEDx speech needed more preparation. In fact, She informed me that most people who take my approach bomb on stage. She could have judged me for being naïve or egotistical. Instead, she assumed positive intent and said, *"How would you like to learn a new skill?"*

The idea of strengthening a skill I lacked got me hooked. I did try out and of course, that TEDx talk is out there in the internet world now. And it has led to many opportunities that simply would not have existed had I made the slightly different choice to respond more aggressively when she asked me to move my car.

I will never know of the opportunities and moments I missed when I decided to take things personally and react defensively for all those years.

When we are moving at the speed of light, even the tiniest infraction can send us off course and ricocheting into missed opportunities or unnecessary breakdowns. Suddenly, our own actions keep us from implementing our ideas and getting important things done. We have enough to deal with without getting in our own way by making assumptions that bring on trouble.

With the practice of assuming positive intent, we access our courage and strength to be the one in the relationship who can give the benefit of the doubt. We stop the rush to judgment and take a moment to find out the real story. We avoid the self-fulfilling prophecies that we sometimes create through our own negative energy.

With one simple practice, we become curious. Instead of thinking that we know the other person's intentions, we give them a chance to share with us what they really want. We move into this moment, instead of living out of our past. We build a bridge of trust.

If only it were as simple to master. When we are dealing with many layers of change, it can feel indulgent to take a moment for ourselves—even to take a deep breath. I get it—because I move super-fast and always have a dozen balls in the air. Yet when I take a moment to pause, breathe, and reflect, the outcome is almost always better than it would have been had I forged ahead.

All too often, my own judgments, frustrations, control issues, pains, and anxieties cloud my vision. If I am to see the caring, compassionate, kind, helpful intent of another, I must see past my defensive shields to my own internal strength and clarity. Only then can I see it in another and make different assumptions.

So, here's my question for you: How ready are you to give it a shot?

Before you answer that question, consider what happens to the course of your career and your life if you keep doing what you've always done. Are you on a trajectory that gets you where you want to go, in the way you want to get there?

Taking that pause deeply changed my life. One of the biggest decisions of my life (which involved my husband Russ), was to leave our city life in Charlotte and move to Lake Lure, North Carolina. My career trajectory was definitely on the path I was seeking. Bigger roles, massive bonuses, and a more visible status were on the horizon. Everything I thought I wanted was within my reach.

But my career was costing me my life. Stress-related health problems had started surfacing. My relationships were fraying. My daughter was suicidal and caught in addiction. (How we have come through that is another story. You can follow her journey at www.maneelyconsulting.com.)

A moment of accidentally assuming positive intent allowed me to be curious enough to ask the pivotal question that led to our move. For at least two years, my husband had been trying to get me to buy a lake house. We had looked at so many lakes in the region, and nothing ever seemed quite right. Much to my relief, it was starting to look like we might even sell the boat and settle down like "normal people."

Just when I thought it was over, he raised the topic one day. Instead of my usual assumptions about why he wanted this (and my fear that we would go broke paying for it), I paused, took a deep breath and asked, "Why is this so important to you?"

Well, you could have knocked me over with a feather at the conversation that ensued. He said, "All day long, I work on software and the results don't feel tangible. I love to work with my hands and love to see the results of my hard work." I said

"Well that's exactly why I DON'T want a lake house! After living in this dog-eat-dog world all week, all I want to do on the weekends is read a book, sit on the porch, and watch birds. The last thing I want to do is work on projects all weekend."

His answer showed me just how wrong my assumptions had been. "You don't have to work on projects! I love watching you rest and enjoy yourself on the porch swing or in the hammock."

That's when the assumptions I didn't even know I was making got uncovered. In the world according to me, when Russ was working, I was supposed to be working, too. His idea of heaven was my personal idea of hell.

So, I came back with this question: "You mean, you are ok if you are working and I'm doing something fun, or just relaxing?"

His resounding "Yes!" started us on the journey to moving and probably saved my marriage, my life, and probably my daughter's life as well.

Not only did we move, but I started questioning my assumptions. I came to realize that the strongest thing I could do was to let others tell me what they really thought, rather than assuming it for them. I learned that it's ok to want things for myself, and I owed it to myself to get clear on what that was.

Life is short. There's no time to waste it living out someone else's expectations.

I'm not saying all this to get you to quit your job or to stop caring what the people around you think.

What I *am* saying is this: If you choose to give assuming positive intent a shot, something is going to change in your life. Even a tiny pivot to a new choice can set things off in a different direction.

Doing so will give you opportunities to grow within yourself.

Being able to assume positive intent is a wonderful way to build your internal strength and clarity. When you invest in yourself to build strength and clarify your intentions, you have more power to decide outcomes, even as the outside world gets faster and more chaotic. Developing your inner self-awareness is the real work of assuming positive intent. You cannot see in another what you cannot access in yourself.

That's where "mental strength training" comes in. We need our minds to work *for* us instead of *against* us. We have an incredibly powerful tool in our hands when we learn to master it.

I love this quote from Marcus Aurelius, emperor of Rome from 161 to 180 AD—he sums up life today, which is much as it was in his time:

"When you wake up in the morning, tell yourself: the people I deal with today will be meddling, ungrateful, arrogant, dishonest, jealous, and surly. They are like this because they can't tell good from evil. But I have seen the beauty of good, and the ugliness of evil, and have recognized that the wrongdoer has a nature related to my own — not of the same blood and birth, but the same mind, and possessing a share of the divine. And so none of them can hurt me. No one can implicate me in ugliness. Nor can I feel angry at my relative, or hate him. We were

born to work together like feet, hands and eyes, like the two rows of teeth, upper and lower. To obstruct each other is unnatural. To feel anger at someone, to turn your back on him: these are unnatural."

Assuming positive intent is the quickest path I know to gaining access to your wisdom and strength when the people around you are being human.

As you bring these ideas into your life, remember this: your own assumptions dictate the outcome as much, if not more than the action of the other person in the situation. Each day we face miscommunications, accidental oversights, provocative people, and even those who are out to get us. Every situation presents a new opportunity to take a deep breath, to focus on the path we want—to choose the elegant pivot. And when you choose to pivot, you truly become the co-writer of your life.

I am confident that with these tools and committed practice you will experience a rewarding journey and pen a better story for yourself and for those around you.

QUICK GUIDE TO ASSUMING POSITIVE INTENT

STEP ONE Recognize That You Have a Choice of Which "Wire" to Touch	When someone does something that you are tempted to take personally, remember: It's never personal. Choose to be curious, interested, and caring instead of making it about you.
STEP TWO Pause and Take a Deep Breath	A couple of deep breaths will give you some distance. Give yourself some space before you react
STEP THREE Make Up a Better Story	Instead of making up a story that makes you a victim or the other person a villain, make up a story that makes you both heroes. Make up a story that makes you both stronger.
STEP FOUR Act on That New Story	Act on the story that puts you on the path of where you want to go. Respond rather than react. Stay focused on your path while being aware of potential obstacles.

ACKNOWLEDGMENTS

Every book is the product of a team and this one is no different. I had so many teachers along this crooked and harrowing journey, and ironically, many were the people whose names I will never know. So I'll start by thanking all of the people I encountered in the airport, taxi rides, and grocery stores. Then there were the hundreds of co-workers—more than I can possibly remember, much less name.

It takes a great editor to make a great book and I couldn't ask for better than Tina Wolfe. Several years ago, she took me to lunch and asked to be involved in helping me share my message to the world. Over that lunch meeting (which involved some extraordinary homemade potato chips overlooking Lake Lure), she shared her experience in editing and launching books. I politely told her I would consider her offer. Several months later, I found myself saying out loud "I'm going to write a book." Some of that courage came from knowing who I could ask for help. This book is eminently better for having had her thoughtful eye throughout.

As I stated above, there were hundreds of people I worked with who taught me what to do -and to not do—in navigating the corporate world. Vernon Roberts gave me the gift of seeing the best in me, even when I was at my worst. Here's how he put it when I shared these stories with him: "I never thought that you were a bitch. I just knew you were driven. I thought of you like the wind. When we were with you I had to decide if you were a breeze that could fill our sails to move us along or a tornado. In the latter case, run for cover. But that was just who you were and I admired the whole person." If that isn't assuming positive intent in a nutshell, I don't know what is.

Steve Snyder saw me through some of my most difficult waters, especially when I wanted to quit on my journey and leave him and his team in a lurch because I was too scared to face the consequences of my actions. I am so grateful for his steady hand as we navigated through extraordinarily difficult resistance and more than our share of bad news. I have no doubt that some of those moments of truth prepared me for the worse that was yet to come.

The first time I met Katy Strei, I realized that I had never met anyone quite like her. It was during my first time as a consultant outside the safe walls of employment. She asked for things with a specificity I had never experienced. The petulant child in me wondered why she didn't trust me to bring her back what she needed. Soon I discovered that she had a magical way of setting me and my colleagues up for success. She modeled assuming positive intent in virtually every interaction. Watching her navigate the world was a masterclass in holding people to their highest intentions.

Then I had the opportunity to work with Sister Lillian

Murphy. None of the filters in my Yellow Volkswagen world included a nun who ran a multibillion dollar real estate company. Yet here she was, leading an organization as CEO that served important human needs and economic needs at the same time. Over the ten plus years of working with her and her team, I saw a leader who embraced assuming positive intent as a core value at the root of almost every other value. At her funeral in August 2019, her friend and colleague Helen Dunlap passed out buttons for all of us to wear: "Presume Positive Intent." Sr. Lillian, I will never forget you.

Of course, I must thank all the characters, real and imagined (I'm talking to you, Fighting Francis), that I wrote about in *The Elegant Pivot*. Every story is true, although I did take some license in disguising settings and identities. For everyone involved in these stories, I thank you deeply!

One of the stories I will never disguise is that of my daughter Jen Maneely and her journey through addiction. My behavior early in her life—let's call it my "tornado years"—most certainly contributed to her need to hide and numb her feelings through any means available. When all else failed, she turned to drugs. Her story could have ended so very differently, yet she persevered and celebrates 14 years clean at the time of this publication. Her journey through addiction offered an incredible lesson for me. Today she works closely with parents of addicts to help them understand the ways they unknowingly contribute to the patterns of addiction and she shows them the simple (yet not easy) ways they can break those patterns with love and compassionate boundaries. Her skills as a coach have, in many ways, surpassed my own and I could not be more proud of her.

Finally, I am so thankful to my husband Russ Pitts, who has opened me up to so many more possibilities than I ever could have dreamed. We now live a "lake life," where I either water ski, row in my sculling boat, kayak, or hike almost every day and he still does projects, building and fixing things to his heart's content.

RESOURCES

As you have probably guessed by reading this book, my experiments, learning, and failures continue to this day. You can keep up with my "adventures" through *The Coaching Digest*, a weekly newsletter, as well as my podcast titled "Creative Spirits Unleashed. I interview some very interesting people, including business people, athletes and horse trainers. Many of the people mentioned in this book have been on the podcast. It's the best way to get access to my incredible network of coaches and teachers.

Most importantly, with a subscription to *The Coaching Digest*, you get something available only to subscribers: a free digital copy of the companion workbook for *The Elegant Pivot*. Sign up at www.lynncarnes.com.

Recommended Books

The Artist's Way: A Spiritual Path to Higher Creativity, Julia Cameron

The Four Agreements: A Practical Guide to Personal Freedom Meditations, Marcus Aurelius

The Fifth Discipline Fieldbook: Strategies and Tools for Building a Learning Organization, Peter Senge, with Kleiner, Roberts,

Ross and Smith

The Art of Learning: An Inner Journey to Optimal Performance, Josh Waitzkin

Dear Parents: Strategies to Help Your Loved One Through Addiction, Jennifer Maneely

The Delicate Art: Learn to Say No and Unleash Your Performance, Lynn Carnes

Recommended Programs

Natural Humanship with Bruce Anderson:
http://www.naturesview.us/

The Artist's Way: https://juliacameronlive.com/lifetime/

Unbreakable Boundaries: www.maneelyconsulting.com

Made in the USA
Coppell, TX
28 April 2021